PRE-READING
PIANO SKILL SET
technique

Piano Skill Set: Pre-reading Technique by Phoenix Vera
Copyright © 2024 TT~PT
pianoskillset.com

All Rights Reserved. Printed in U.S.A.

No part of this publication may be reproduced, distributed, or transmitted in any form or by any means, including photocopying, recording, or other electronic or mechanical methods, without the prior written permission of the publisher, except as permitted by U.S. copyright law. For permission requests, contact the author at thetattooedpianoteacher@gmail.com.

PRE-READING
PIANO SKILL SET

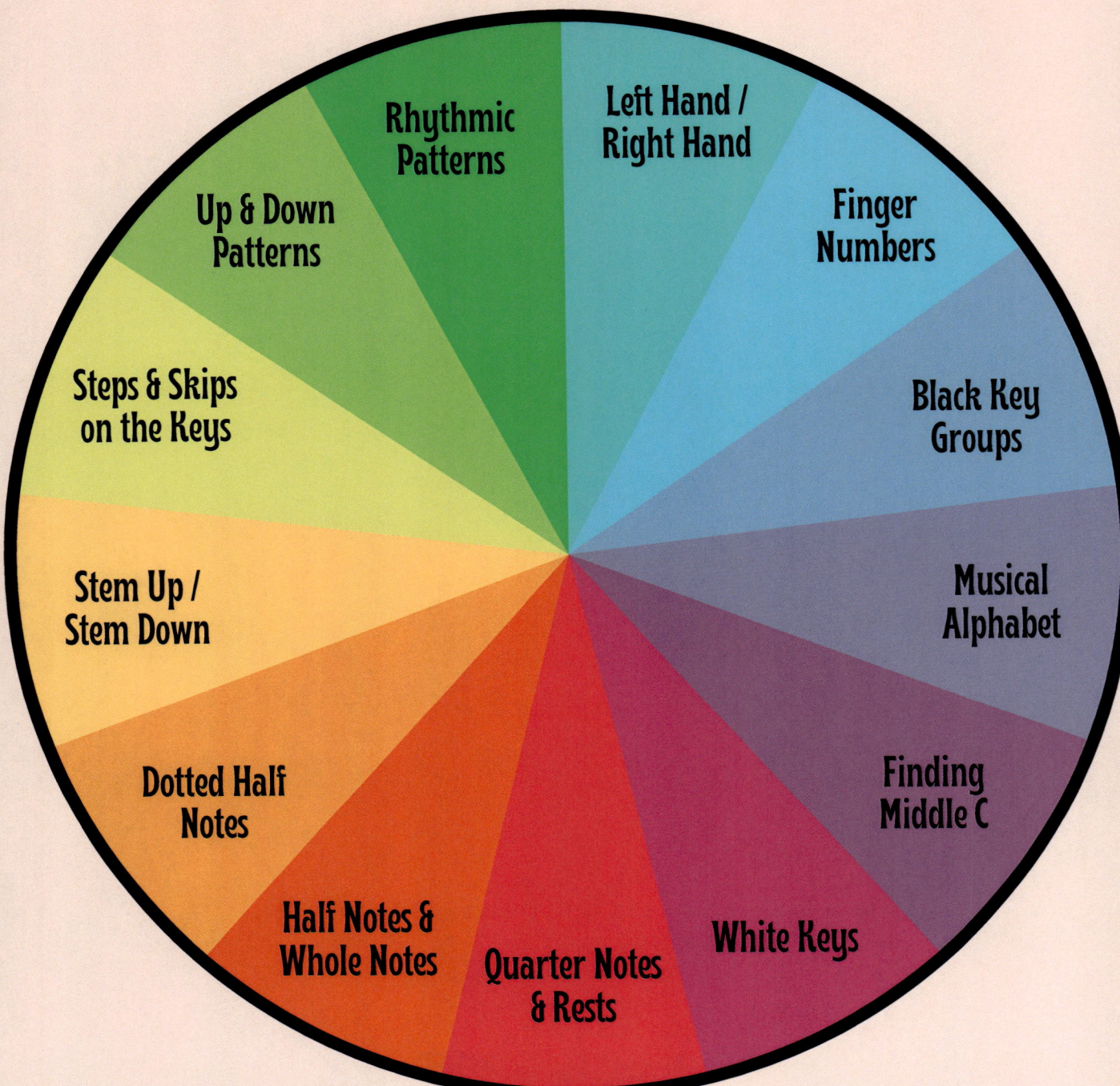

WHY PRE-READING SKILLS?

We all know that note reading skills are vital to becoming a confident, well-rounded pianist. By establishing strong pre-reading skills, we properly prepare students to absorb reading notes on the grand staff when they are ready.

Imagine learning a foreign language while still mastering basic reading and writing skills in your native language? That would make things quite difficult! You might feel a bit overwhelmed. Focusing on pre-reading skills in the beginning will actually save time and frustration in the future for our young musicians. This is time well spent. Happy teaching!

PRE-READING
PIANO SKILL SET
technique

LIST OF PRE-READING SKILLS

1	LEFT HAND / RIGHT HAND	PAGE 5
2	FINGER NUMBERS	PAGE 7
3	BLACK KEY GROUPS	PAGE 10
4	MUSICAL ALPHABET	PAGE 27
5	FINDING MIDDLE C	PAGE 29
6	WHITE KEYS	PAGE 30
7	QUARTER NOTES & RESTS	PAGE 33
8	HALF NOTES & WHOLE NOTES	PAGE 35
9	DOTTED HALF NOTES	PAGE 38
10	STEM UP / STEM DOWN	PAGE 41
11	STEPS & SKIPS ON THE KEYS	PAGE 45
12	UP & DOWN STEPWISE PATTERNS	PAGE 51
13	RHYTHMIC PATTERNS	PAGE 52

HOW TO USE

PRE-READING
PIANO SKILL SET
technique

NEW SKILL
Light bulb pages indicate you'll be learning a brand new skill. After all, that's why you're here! Pay extra close attention and memorize any information shown on a light bulb page...you'll need it in the upcoming pages.

RHYTHM ACTIVITY

Grab a metronome when you see the metronome! Often we'll try out a new skill in its simplest form before applying it to a full song. Have a parent or teacher set a metronome to a slow pace. Read the directions carefully for each activity.

FINGER SKILLS
In this book, we'll spend lots of time perfecting finger independence, hand coordination, and new patterns. When you see the thumbs up, you know you'll be focusing on a very specific skill. Take your time and carefully master these pages before moving on.

SONGS

Special songs throughout this book will help you apply the skills you are working on in real life musical situations. Each song tells its own little story and gives you a chance to rise to the challenge after working on new skills!

GAME TIME
After all of your learning and hard work, it's time for a more relaxed review. Dice pages feature a quick music game you can play with a teacher, parent, sibling, or friend.

MASTERY

These pages will challenge your brain and your hands. Think of these as a "final test" on a skill before moving on to something new. Plan to work long and hard on mastery pages. Your success on these pages will let you know you're right on target!

WRITING ACTIVITY
Grab your pencil whenever you spot the pencil! Although you won't have a lot of writing activities in this book, it's still great to quiz the brain every so often. Use only pencil and read all directions very carefully before starting each activity.

LEFT HAND / RIGHT HAND

NEW SKILL 1

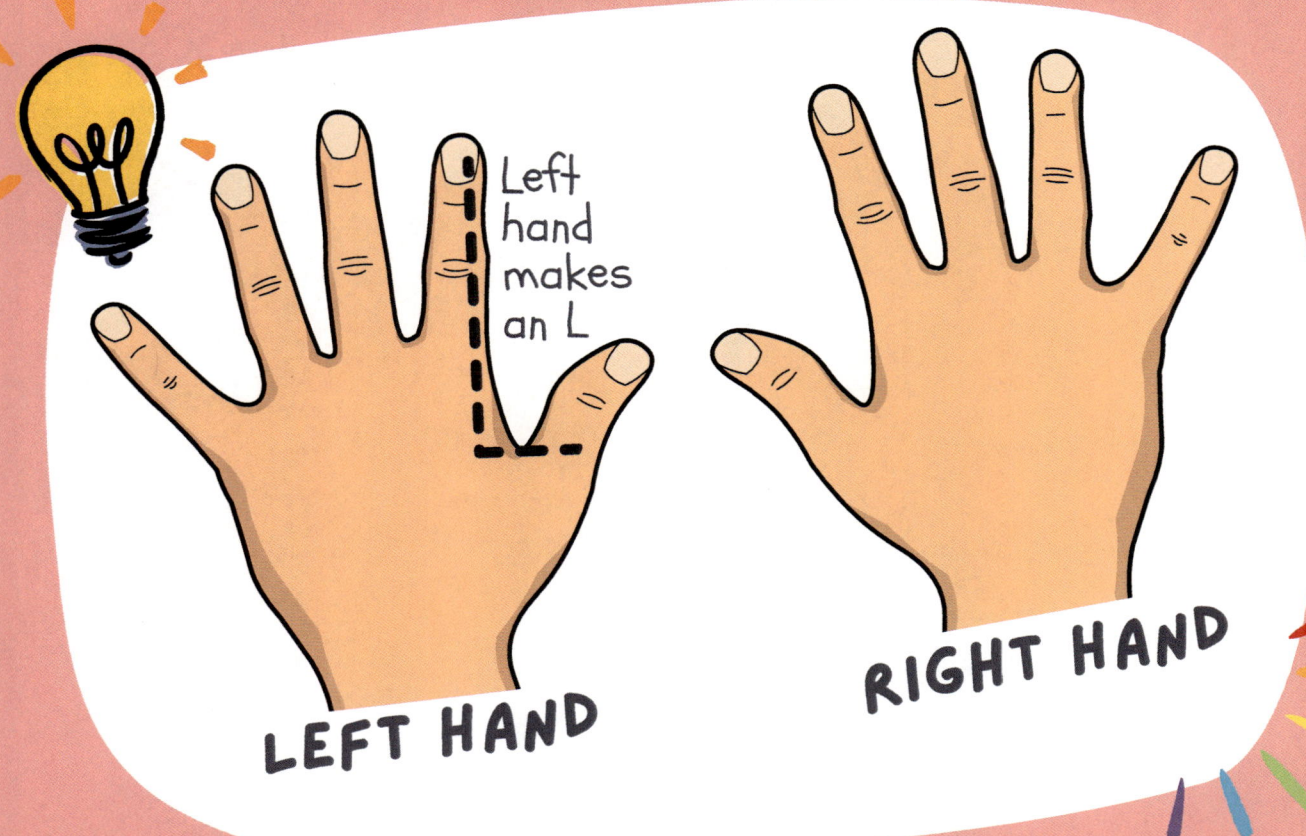

Left hand makes an L

LEFT HAND   RIGHT HAND

YOUR TURN: TAP THE PATTERN

LEFT	LEFT	RIGHT	RIGHT
LEFT	RIGHT	LEFT	RIGHT
RIGHT	RIGHT	RIGHT	LEFT
RIGHT	LEFT	LEFT	RIGHT
LEFT	RIGHT	BOTH!	BOTH!

LET'S PLAY: FAST HANDS

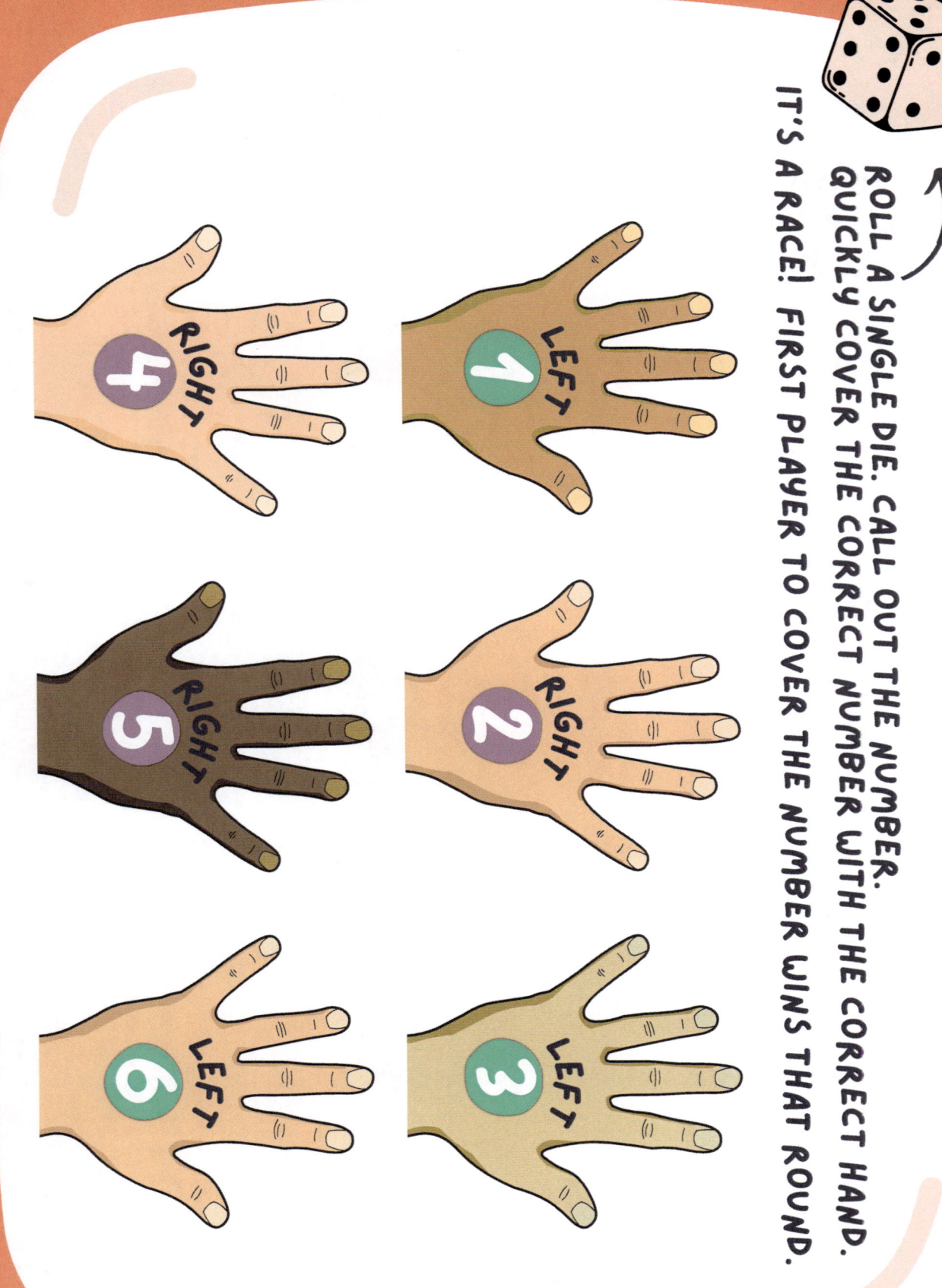

ROLL A SINGLE DIE. CALL OUT THE NUMBER. QUICKLY COVER THE CORRECT NUMBER WITH THE CORRECT HAND. IT'S A RACE! FIRST PLAYER TO COVER THE NUMBER WINS THAT ROUND.

FINGER NUMBERS

NEW SKILL 2

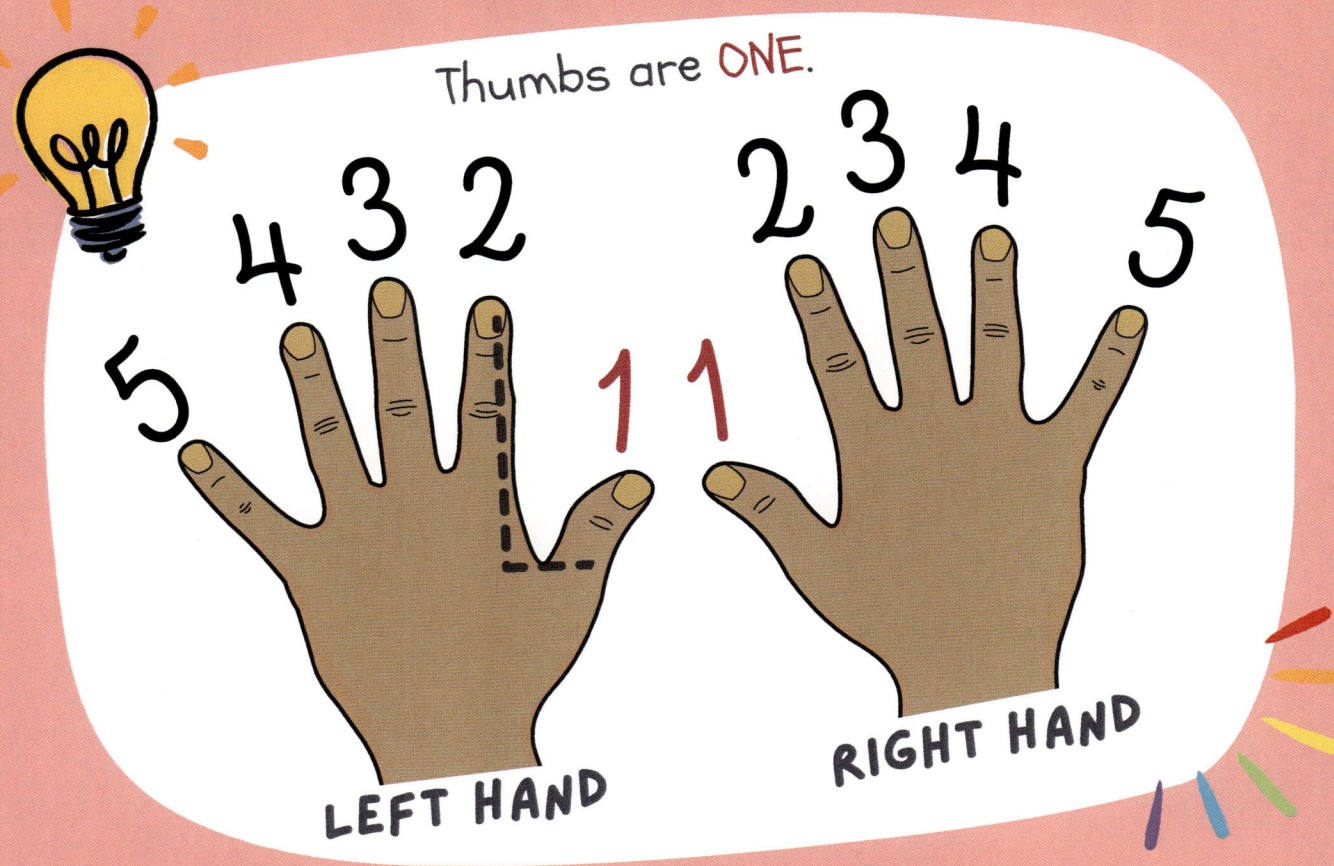

Thumbs are ONE.

LEFT HAND   RIGHT HAND

YOUR TURN: TOUCH EACH NUMBER WITH THE CORRECT FINGER

TOUCH EACH NUMBER WITH THE CORRECT FINGER

RIGHT 2	LEFT 3	LEFT 1	RIGHT 5
RIGHT 1	RIGHT 4	LEFT 2	RIGHT 3
LEFT 5	RIGHT 2	RIGHT 1	LEFT 4
LEFT 3	RIGHT 5	RIGHT 4	LEFT 2

TOUCH EACH SET OF NUMBERS WITH THE CORRECT FINGERS

LEFT 3	LEFT 2	RIGHT 1	RIGHT 5
LEFT 3	LEFT 1	RIGHT 2	RIGHT 4
LEFT 5	LEFT 4	RIGHT 3	RIGHT 5
LEFT 4	LEFT 1	RIGHT 2	RIGHT 5

BLACK KEY GROUPS

NEW SKILL 3

Black keys are in groups of TWO and THREE.

GROUP OF 2 | GROUP OF 3 | GROUP OF 2 | GROUP OF 3 | GROUP OF 2

YOUR TURN:

USING LEFT HAND FINGERS 3 AND 2, PLAY ALL GROUPS OF 2 BLACK KEYS.

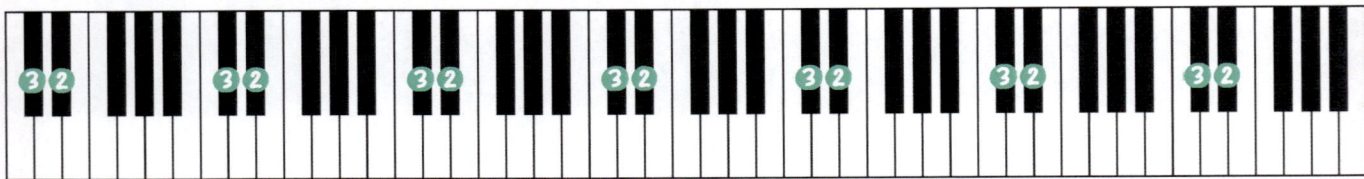

USING RIGHT HAND FINGERS 2, 3 AND 4, PLAY ALL GROUPS OF 3 BLACK KEYS.

RIGHT HAND PLAY EVERY DAY

     move up to the next group of
                                                                    2 black keys to the right

Right   hand   play

     move up again

ever   –   y   day.

     move up again

Don't   de –   lay.

 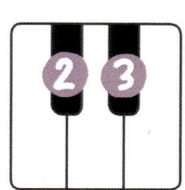 

Start   to –   day!

LEFT HAND PLAY EVERY DAY

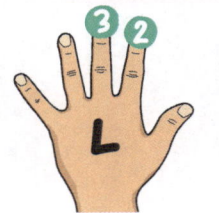

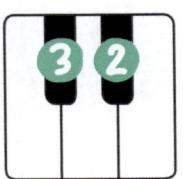 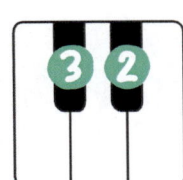 

Left   hand   play

move down to the next group of 2 black keys to the left

ever - y   day.

move down again

Don't   de - lay.

move down again

Start   to - day!

PET STORE WINDOW

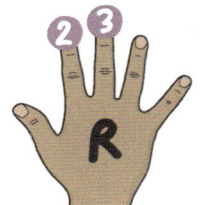

  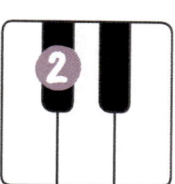  

In   a   pet   store

win — dow   I   can

spy   my   new   best

hold--------------

friend.

CAN WE GO?

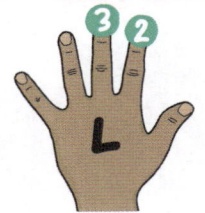

Moth - er,   Fath - er,

can   we   go   to

meet   my   new   best

   hold -------------

friend?

COMING HOME

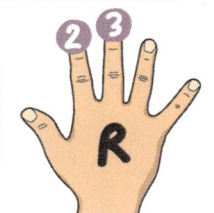

  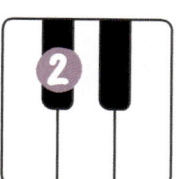 

It's   the   best   day

   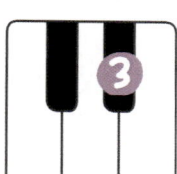

of   my   life.   My

 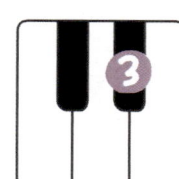  

pup –   py's   com –   ing

home   with   me!

WELCOME HOME

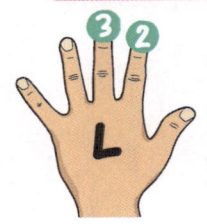  

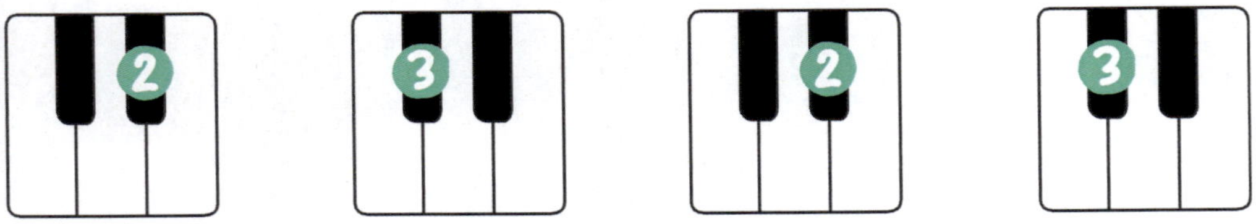

Wel - come   to   your

brand   new   home.   Let's

check   out   all   the

hold-------------

rooms.

PUPPY STEPS

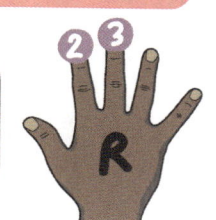

Start s l o w l y - - - - - -

  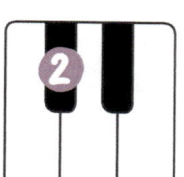   hold--

One   paw   through   the   door.

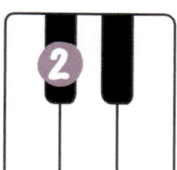  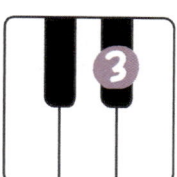   hold--

Slow - ly   sneak - ing   in.

A little f a s t e r - - - - - - -

 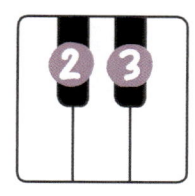  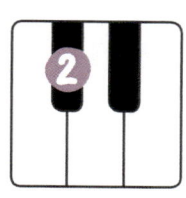 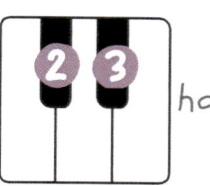 hold--

Sniff   a - round   the   floor.

And now quite f a s t! - - - - - - -

   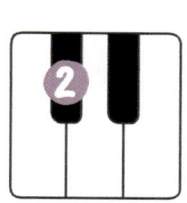  hold--

Hap - py   pup - py   spins.

2 BLACK KEY MASTERY

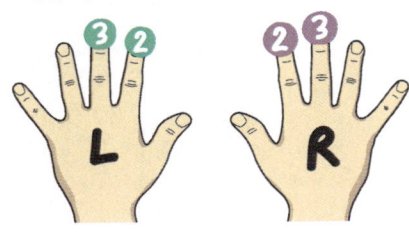

USING BOTH HANDS AT THE SAME TIME, PRACTICE JUMPING FROM A GROUP OF 2 BLACK KEYS TO THE NEXT GROUP OF 2 BLACK KEYS.

MAKE UP A RHYTHM AND CREATE YOUR OWN SONG USING THIS PATTERN.

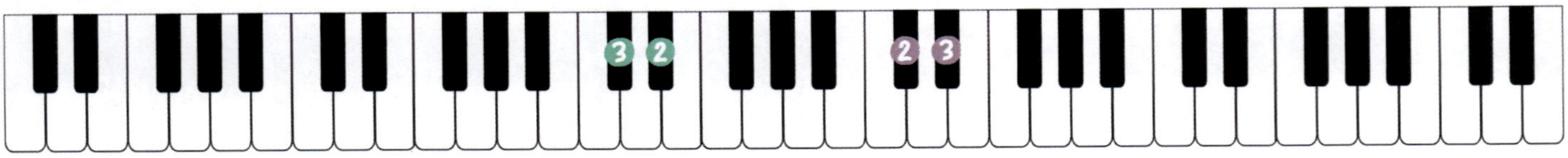

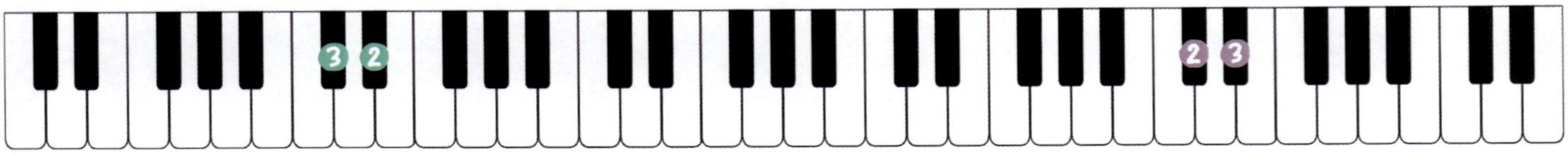

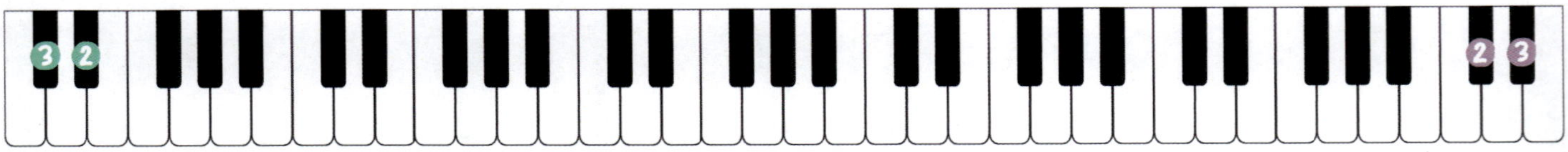

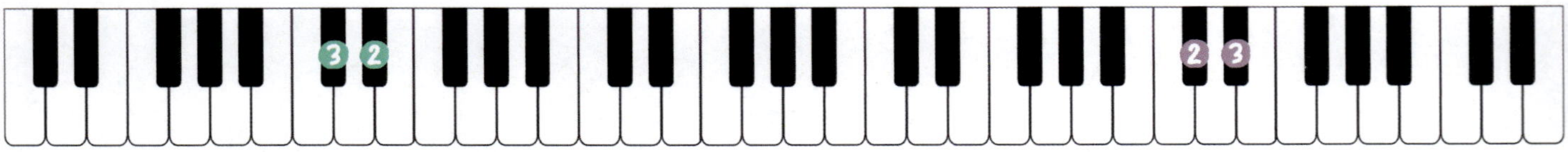

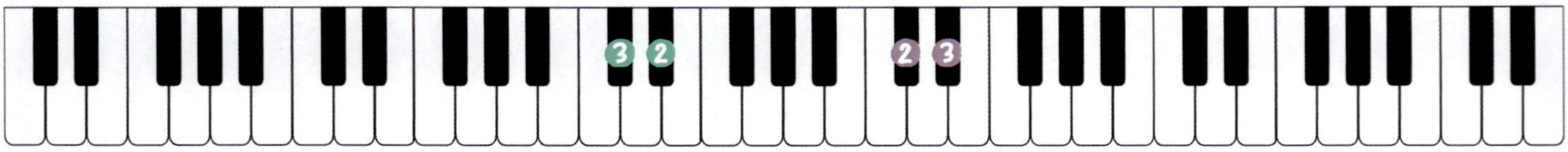

RIGHT HAND PLAY EVERY DAY

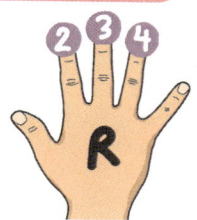

  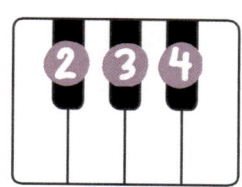   move up to the next group of 3 black keys to the right

Right   hand   play

     move up again

ever – y   day.

  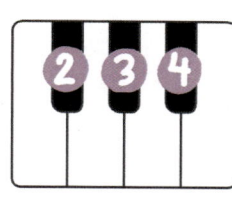   move up again

Don't   de – lay.

Start   to – day!

LEFT HAND PLAY EVERY DAY

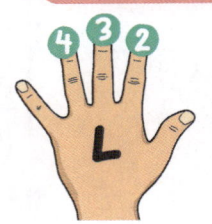

     move down to the next group of 3 black keys to the left

Left   hand   play

  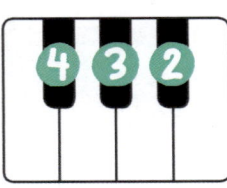   move down again

ever — y   day.

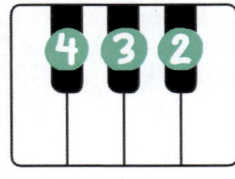  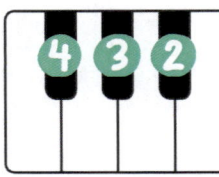   move down again

Don't   de — lay.

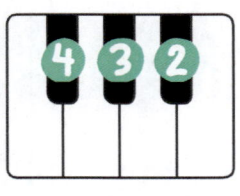 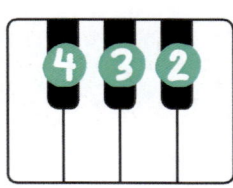 

Start   to — day!

THREE CATS

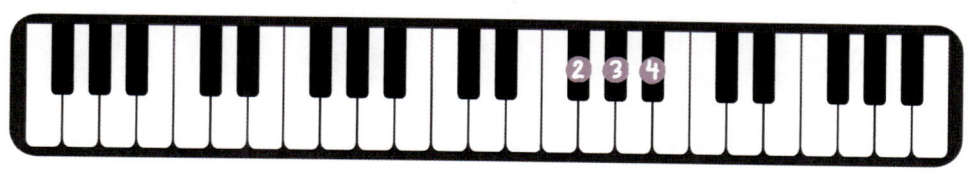
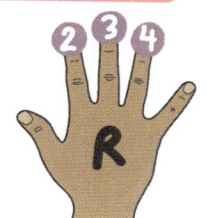

One   is   fluf - fy,

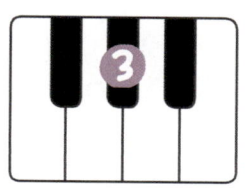  

one   is   smooth,

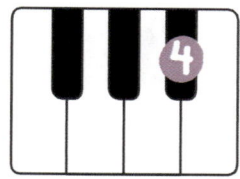  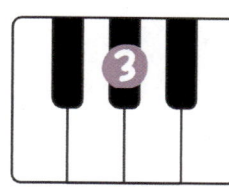 

one   me - ows   when

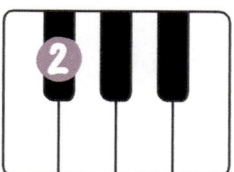  

she   wants   food.

FLUFFY

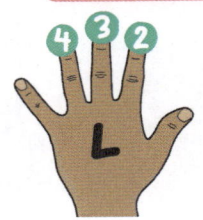 

Fluf – fy,   Fluf – fy,

can't   you   see?

 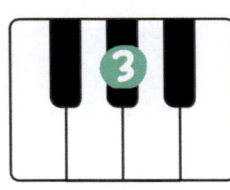 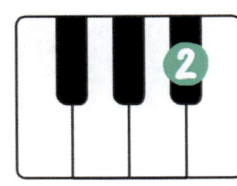 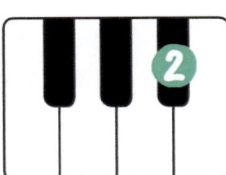

You're   the   soft – est

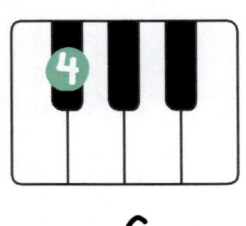   

of   the   three.

CALICO

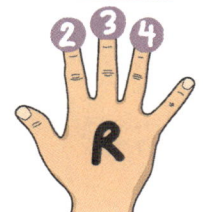

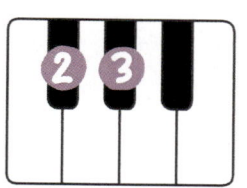   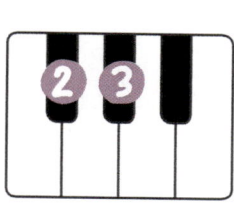 

Mul – ti   col – ored

short – haired   cat.

Cal – i – co   loves

to   be   pet.

THE LOUD ONE

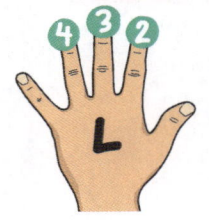

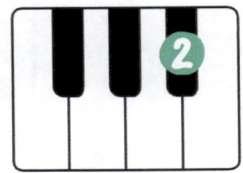   

Purr — ing loud — ly

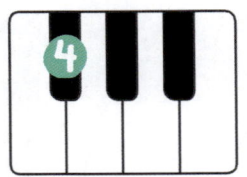  

all night long.

  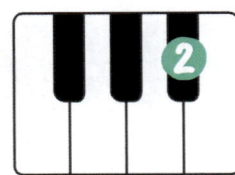 

Yowl — ing, meow — ing

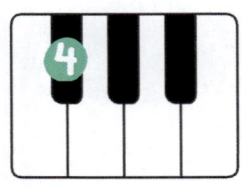  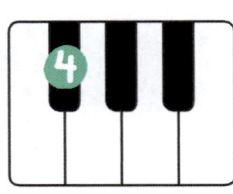 

is her song.

CAT TRIO

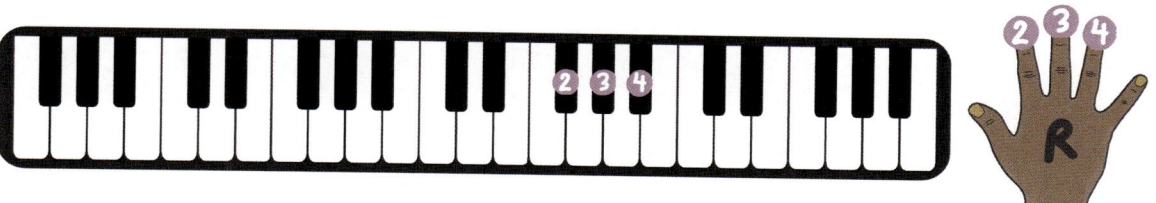

Fluf   –   fy,   Queen   and

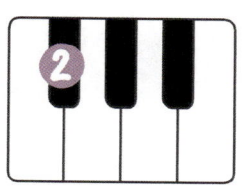   

Cal   –   i   –   co.

"Me   –   ow,   –   me   ow."

 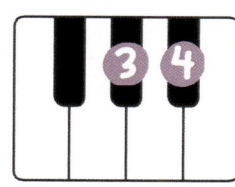 

Cat   tri   –   o.

3 BLACK KEY MASTERY

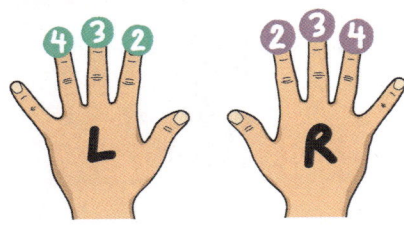

USING BOTH HANDS AT THE SAME TIME, PRACTICE JUMPING FROM A GROUP OF 3 BLACK KEYS TO THE NEXT GROUP OF 3 BLACK KEYS.

MAKE UP A RHYTHM AND CREATE YOUR OWN SONG USING THIS PATTERN.

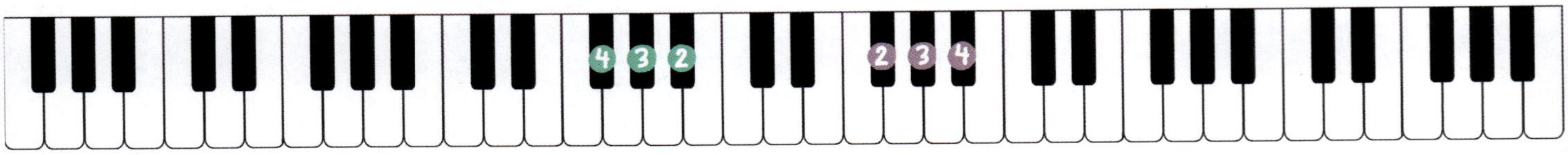

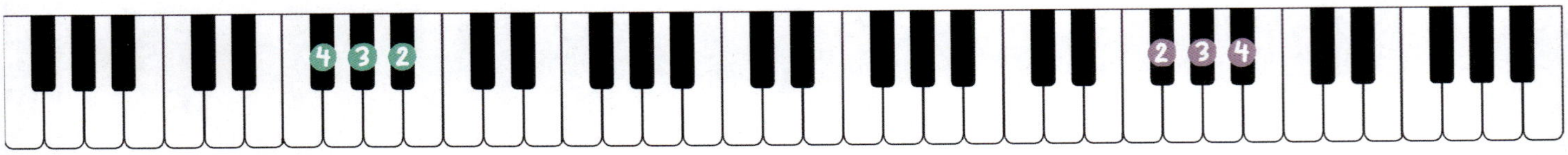

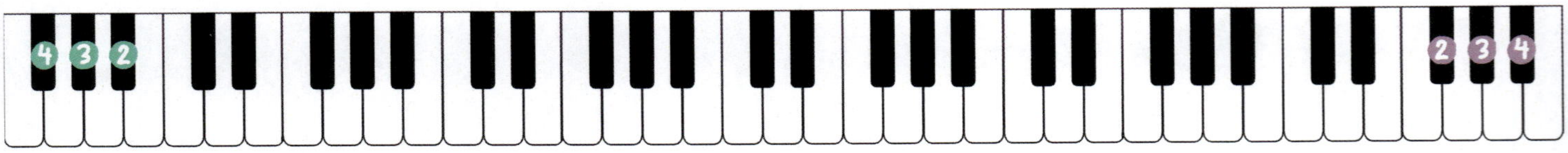

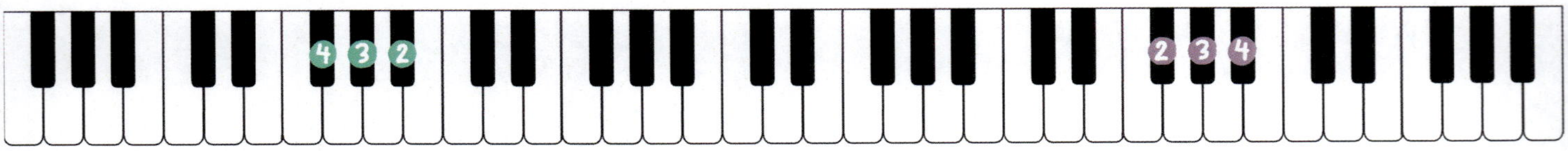

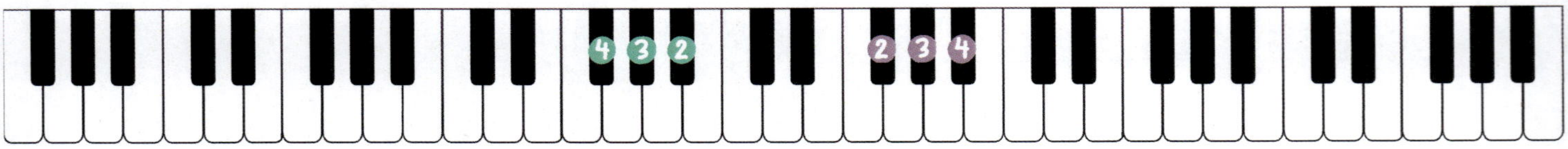

MUSICAL ALPHABET   NEW SKILL 4   27

THE MUSICAL ALPHABET

A B C D E F G A

After G, we start again with A.

YOUR TURN:

YOUR TEACHER WILL HELP YOU FIND THE "A" KEY.

SAY AND PLAY EACH LETTER OF THE MUSICAL ALPHABET AS YOU MOVE UP THE KEYS ONE BY ONE.

Remember that A comes after G.

FINDING MIDDLE C

NEW SKILL 5

Find a group of TWO black keys. See how C is found just to the left?

MIDDLE C is the C closest to the middle of the keyboard

YOUR TURN:

FIND EVERY GROUP OF 2 BLACK KEYS ON YOUR PIANO.

GO TO THE LEFT AND FIND EACH C!

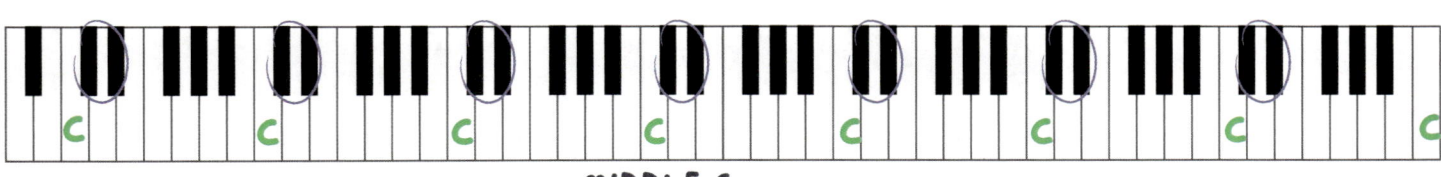

MIDDLE C

PLAY MIDDLE C ONCE FOR EVERY YEAR YOU'VE BEEN ALIVE!

WHITE KEYS

NEW SKILL 6

Find a group of THREE black keys. See how F is found just to the left?

C IS FOUND BY THE 2 BLACK KEY GROUP.
F IS FOUND BY THE 3 BLACK KEY GROUP.

YOUR TURN:

FIND EVERY GROUP OF 3 BLACK KEYS ON YOUR PIANO.

GO TO THE LEFT AND FIND EACH F!

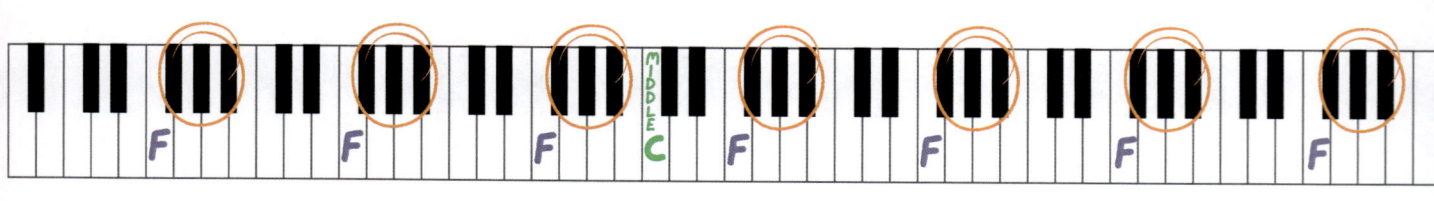

PLAY EVERY F FROM RIGHT TO LEFT.

FIND THE WHITE KEYS

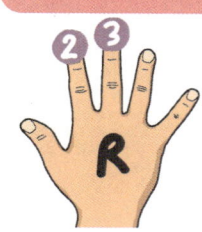

STARTING ON THE LEFT, PLAY EVERY GROUP OF 2 BLACK KEYS FOLLOWED BY THE WHITE KEY SHOWN.

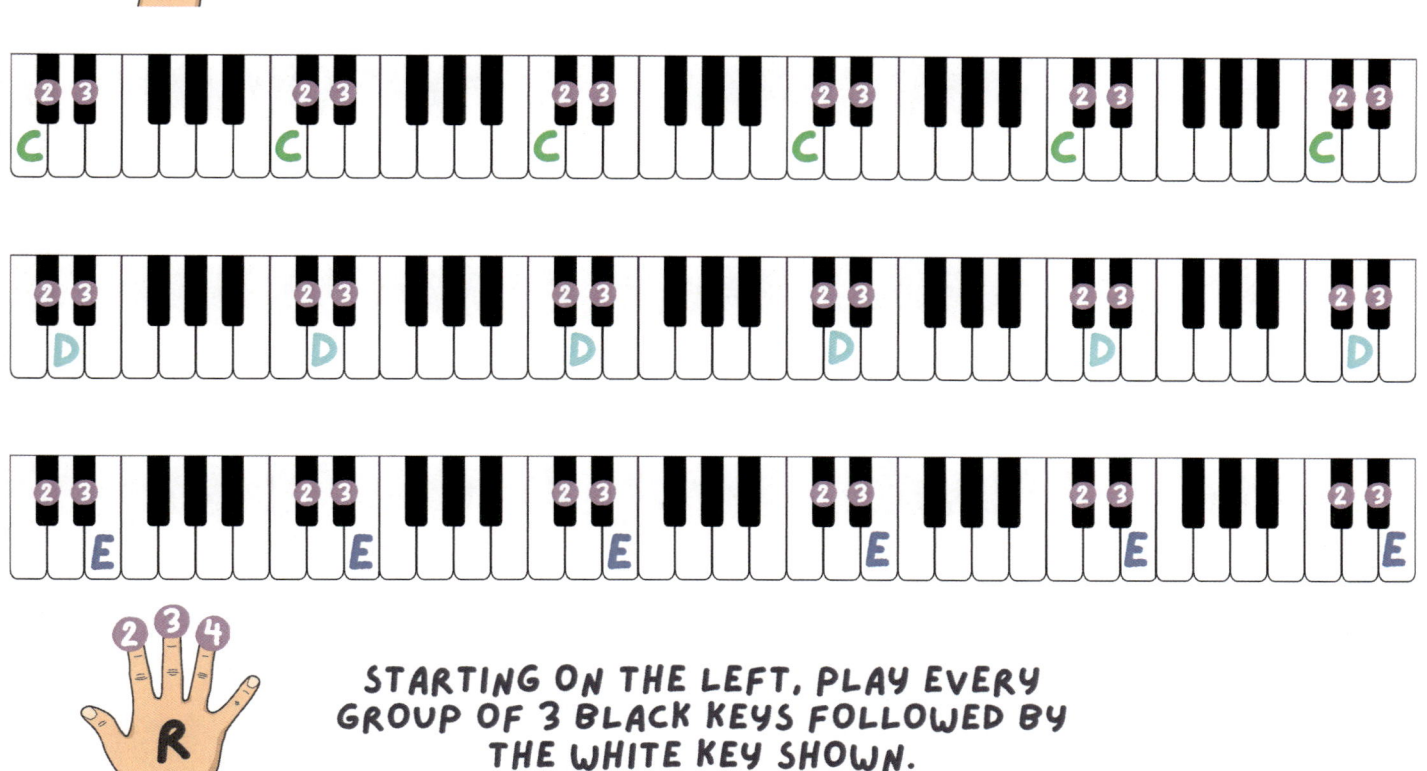

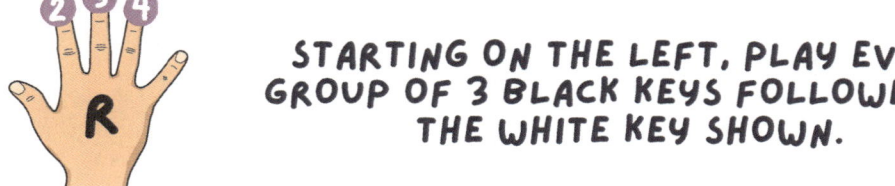

STARTING ON THE LEFT, PLAY EVERY GROUP OF 3 BLACK KEYS FOLLOWED BY THE WHITE KEY SHOWN.

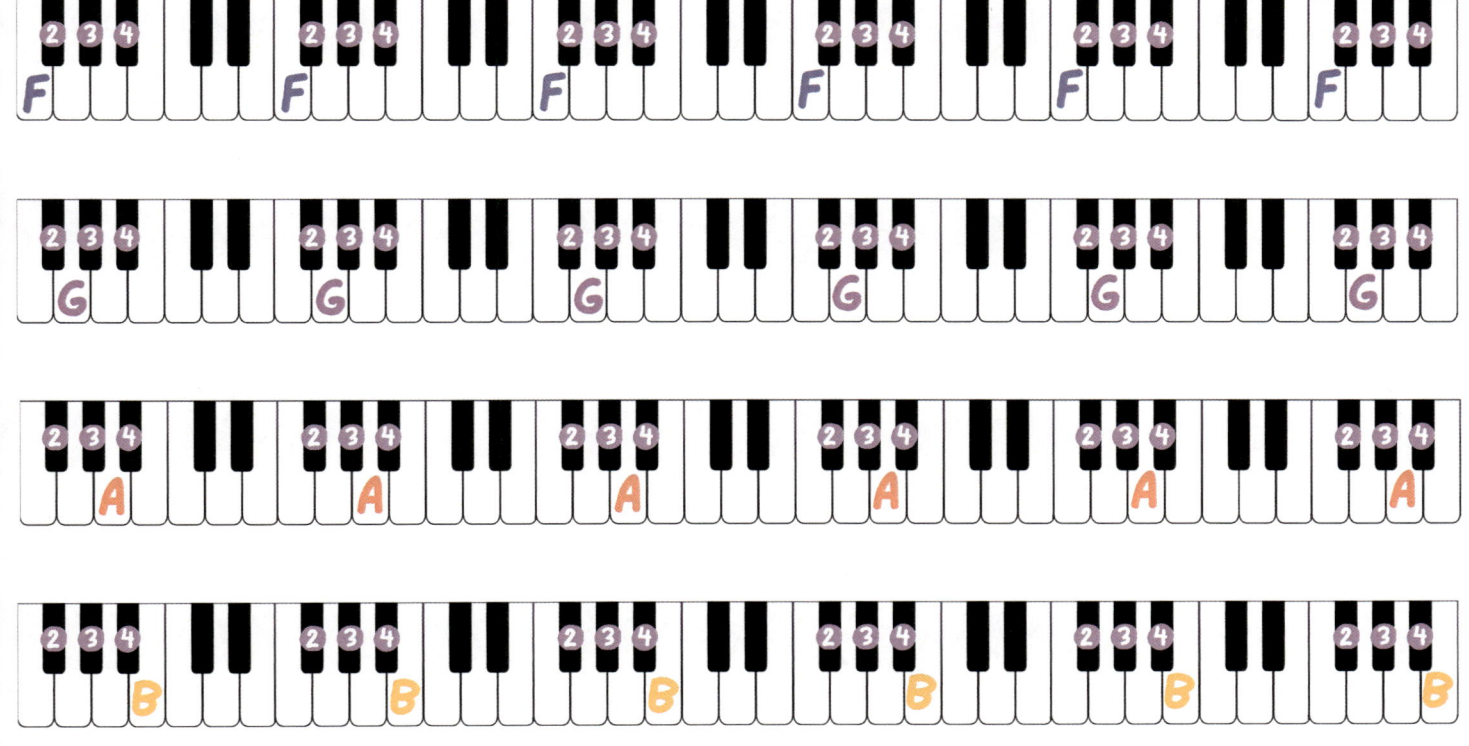

LET'S PLAY: THIS, THIS, AND THAT

ROLL A DIE THREE TIMES.

FIRST ROLL TELLS YOU THE KEY:

⚀ C	⚁ D	⚂ E
⚃ F	⚄ G	⚅ A

SECOND ROLL TELLS YOU THE FINGER:

⚀ 1	⚁ 2	⚂ 3
⚃ 4	⚄ 5	⚅ ROLL AGAIN

THIRD ROLL TELLS YOU HOW MANY TIMES:

⚀ 1x	⚁ 2x	⚂ 3x
⚃ 4x	⚄ 5x	⚅ 6x

ROUND 1  PLAY [ROLL 1 key name] WITH FINGER [ROLL 2 finger number] [ROLL 3 number of times] TIMES

ROUND 2  PLAY [ROLL 1 key name] WITH FINGER [ROLL 2 finger number] [ROLL 3 number of times] TIMES

ROUND 3 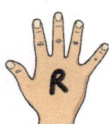 PLAY [ROLL 1 key name] WITH FINGER [ROLL 2 finger number] [ROLL 3 number of times] TIMES

ROUND 4  PLAY [ROLL 1 key name] WITH FINGER [ROLL 2 finger number] [ROLL 3 number of times] TIMES

QUARTER NOTES & RESTS

NEW SKILL 7

QUARTER NOTE
ONE BEAT OF SOUND

QUARTER REST
ONE BEAT OF SILENCE

SAY "quarter note gets ONE beat."

YOUR TURN:

TAP OR CLAP THE RHYTHM.

PLAY EACH RHYTHM ON THE KEY THAT MATCHES THE FIRST LETTER OF EACH WORD. (EXAMPLE: ALLIGATOR ON "A")

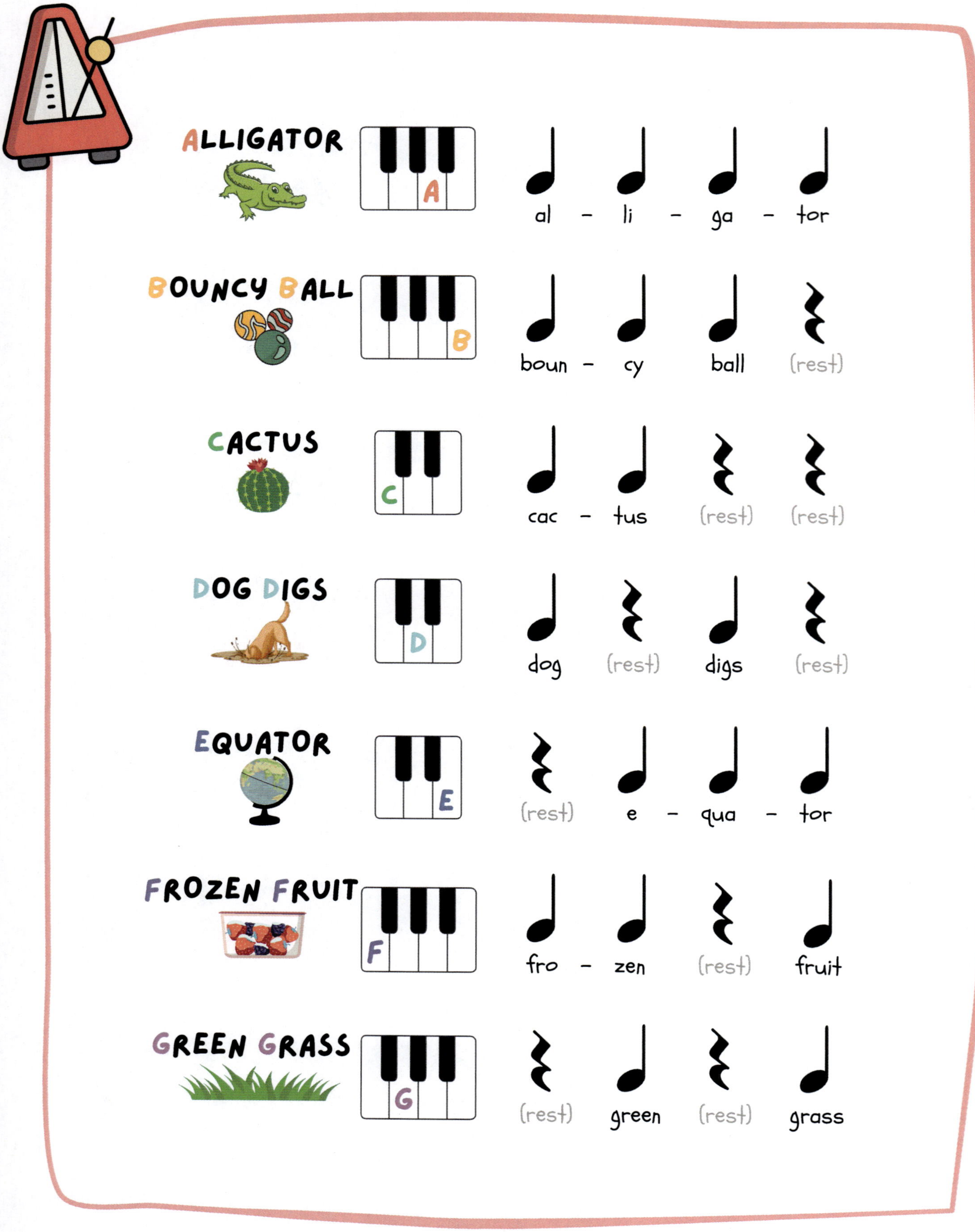

ALLIGATOR   ♩ ♩ ♩ ♩
al – li – ga – tor

BOUNCY BALL 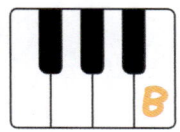 ♩ ♩ ♩ 𝄽
boun – cy ball (rest)

CACTUS   ♩ ♩ 𝄽 𝄽
cac – tus (rest) (rest)

DOG DIGS   ♩ 𝄽 ♩ 𝄽
dog (rest) digs (rest)

EQUATOR   𝄽 ♩ ♩ ♩
(rest) e – qua – tor

FROZEN FRUIT  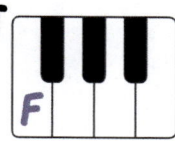 ♩ ♩ 𝄽 ♩
fro – zen (rest) fruit

GREEN GRASS   𝄽 ♩ 𝄽 ♩
(rest) green (rest) grass

HALF NOTES & WHOLE NOTES   NEW SKILL 8

HALF NOTE   WHOLE NOTE

HOLD FOR **2 BEATS**   HOLD FOR **4 BEATS**

SAY "half note gets TWO beats."
SAY "whole note gets FOUR beats."

YOUR TURN:

TAP OR CLAP THE RHYTHM.

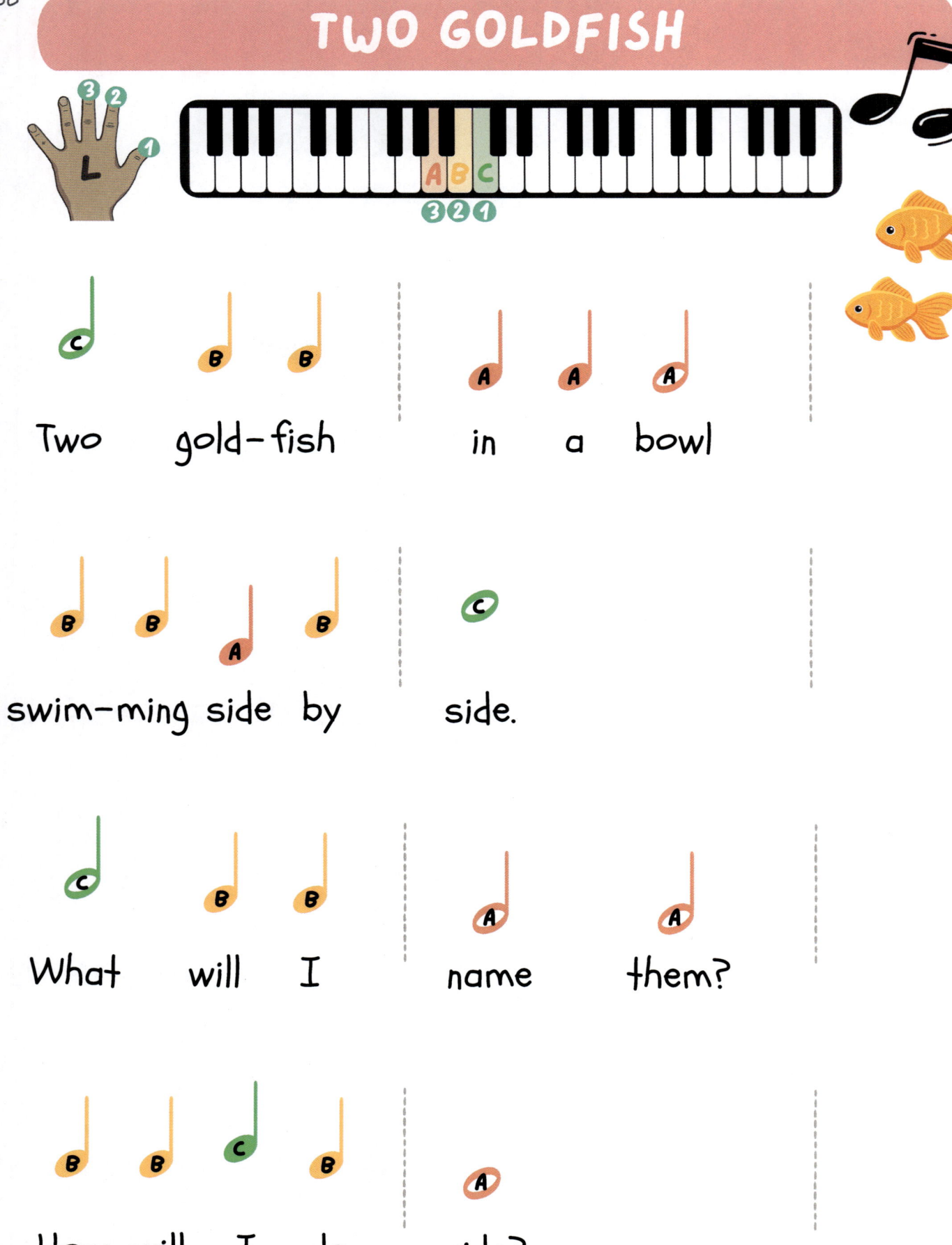

PEOPLE NAMES

C C D D E E
Ro-ger, Her-bert, Su — san,

D D C D E
Har — ri — et and James.

C D D E E
Should my two gold — fish

D D E D C
Live with peo-ple names?

DOTTED HALF NOTES

NEW SKILL 9

DOTTED HALF NOTE

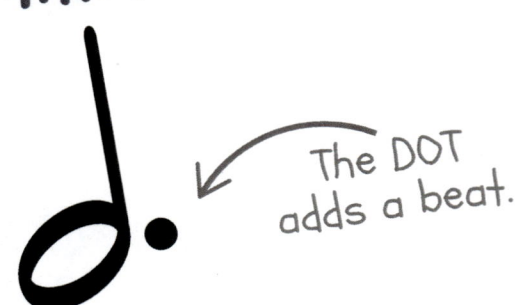

𝅗𝅥. ← The DOT adds a beat.

HOLD FOR 3 BEATS

SAY "dotted half note gets THREE beats."

YOUR TURN:

TAP OR CLAP THE RHYTHM.

PETE SPEAKS

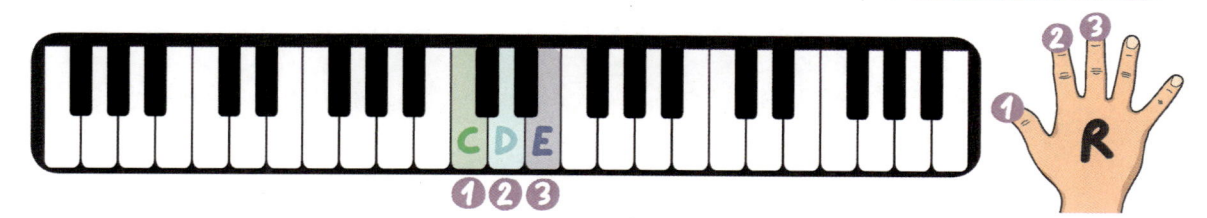

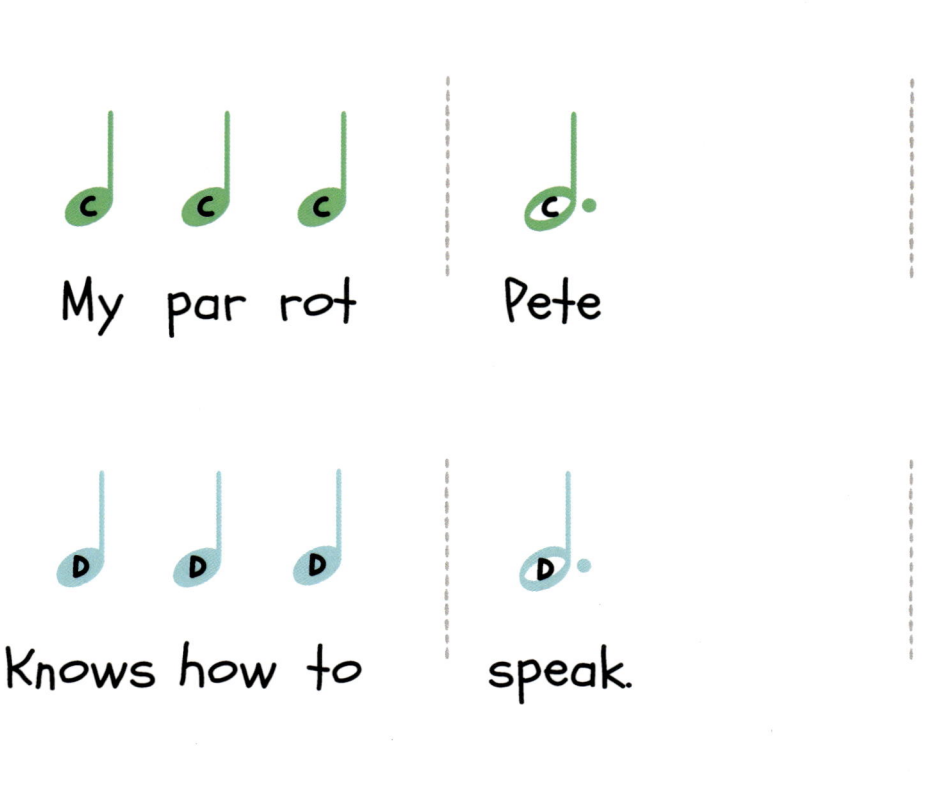

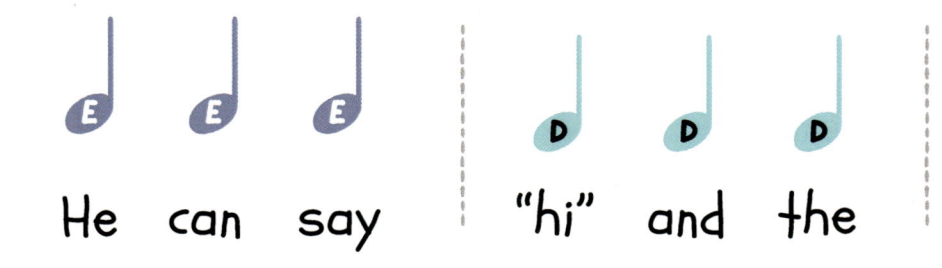

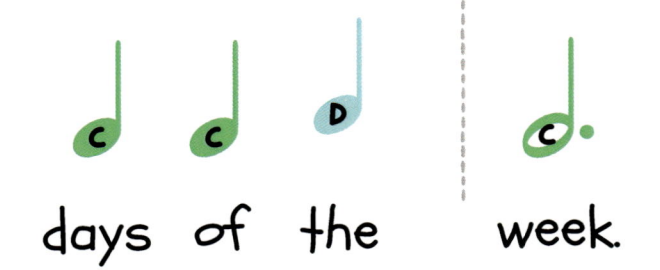

My par rot Pete

Knows how to speak.

He can say "hi" and the

days of the week.

ASK FOR A TREAT

Pete is so smart. He

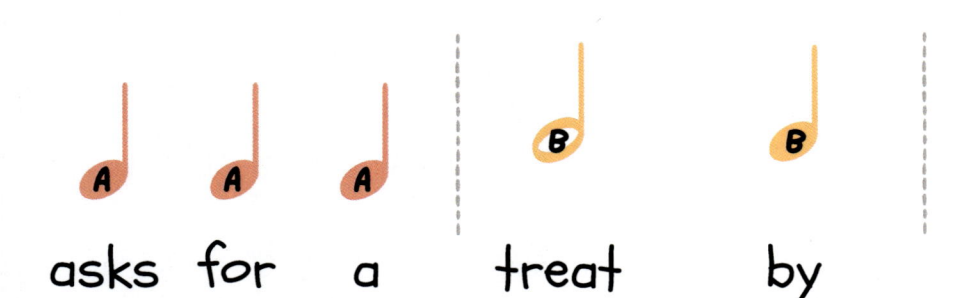

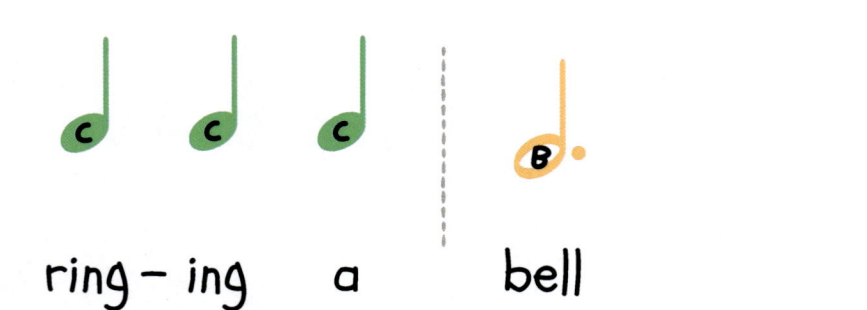

asks for a treat by

ring-ing a bell

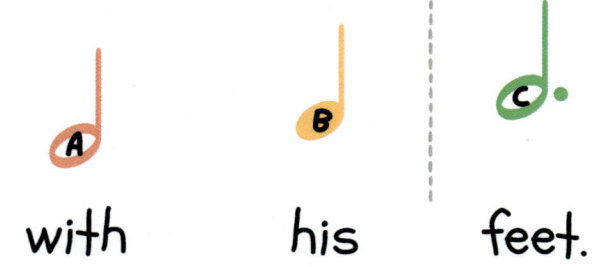

with his feet.

STEM UP / STEM DOWN

NEW SKILL 10 — 41

LEFT HAND
Stem DOWN

RIGHT HAND
Stem UP

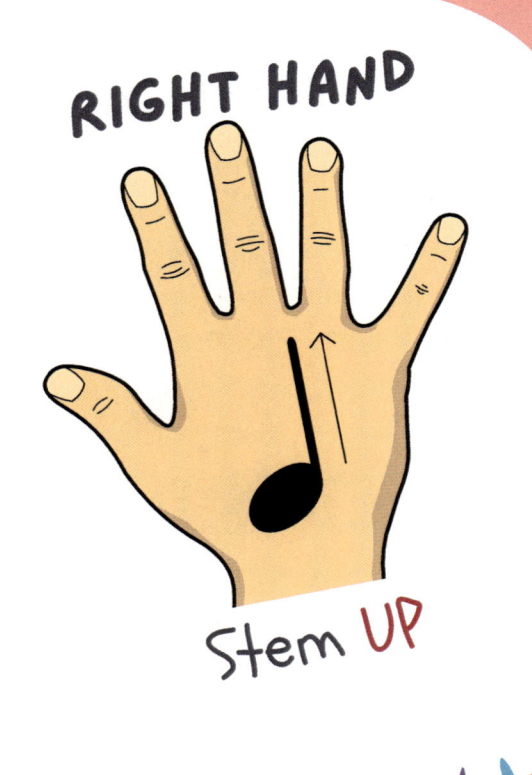

YOUR TURN:

TAP THE RHYTHM USING THE CORRECT HAND(S).

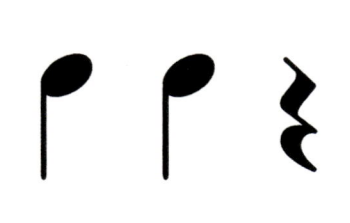

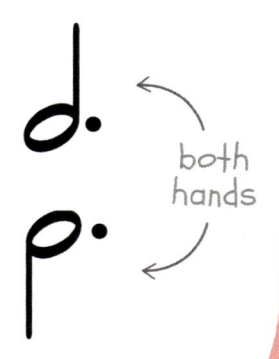

♩ 𝄽 ♩ | 𝅗𝅥. | ♩ ♩ 𝄽 | 𝅗𝅥. / 𝅗𝅥. ← both hands

FAVORITE FOODS

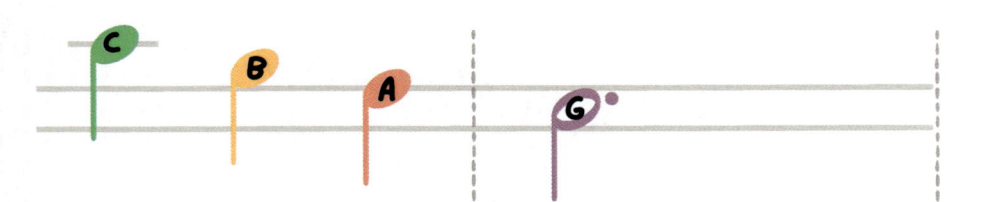

Sun-flow-er seeds,

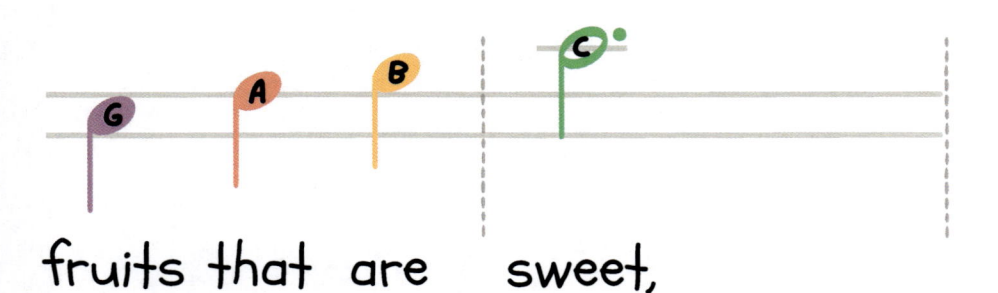

fruits that are sweet,

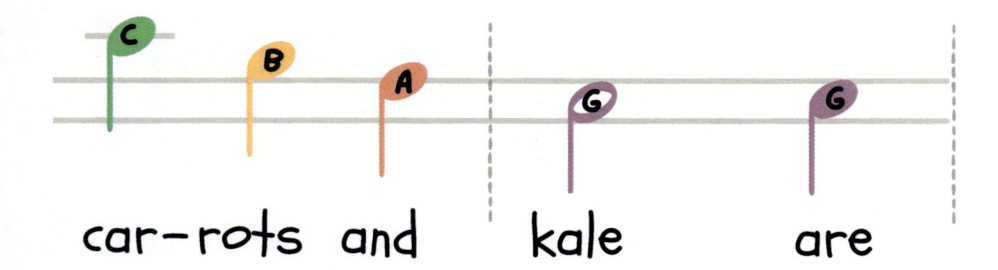

car-rots and kale are

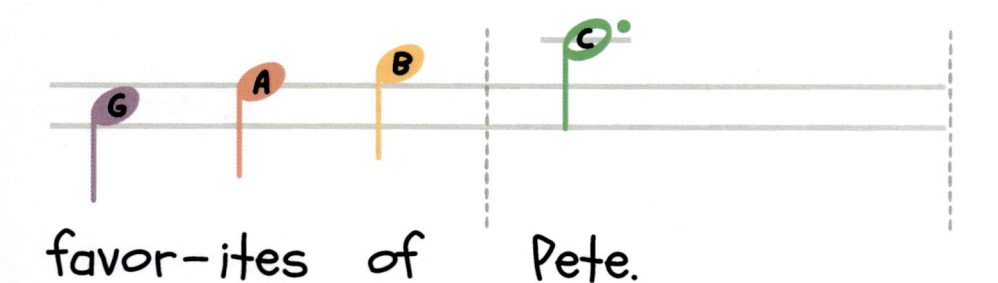

favor-ites of Pete.

PARROT SONG

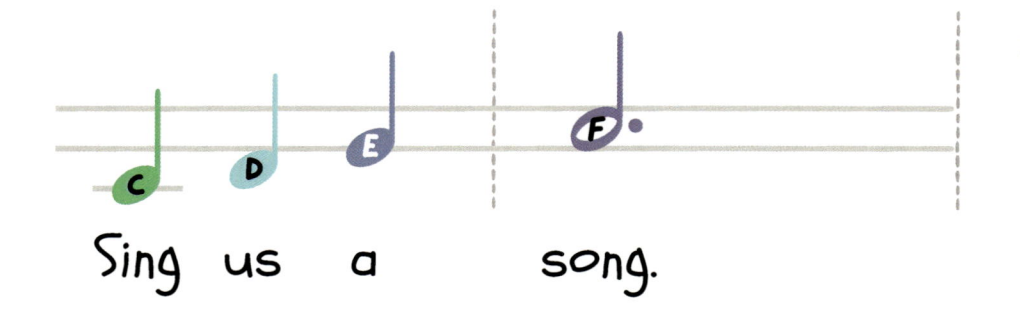

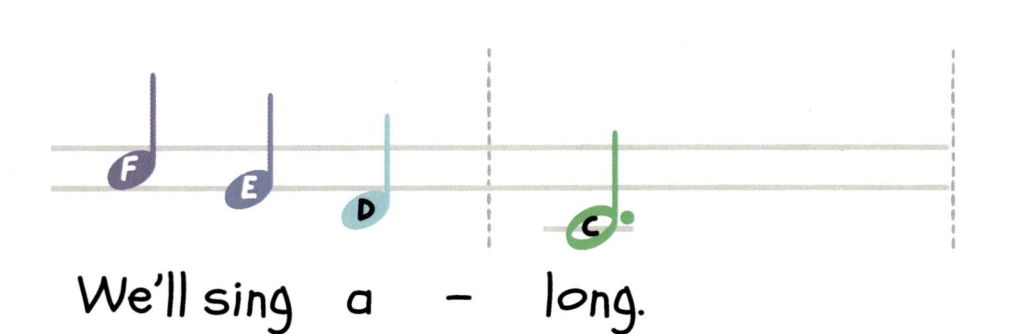

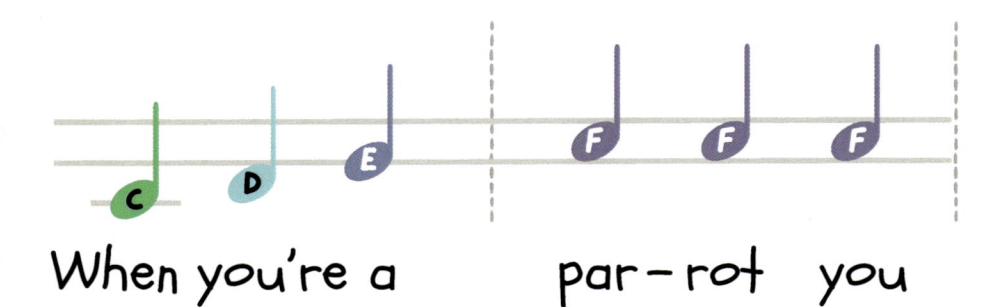

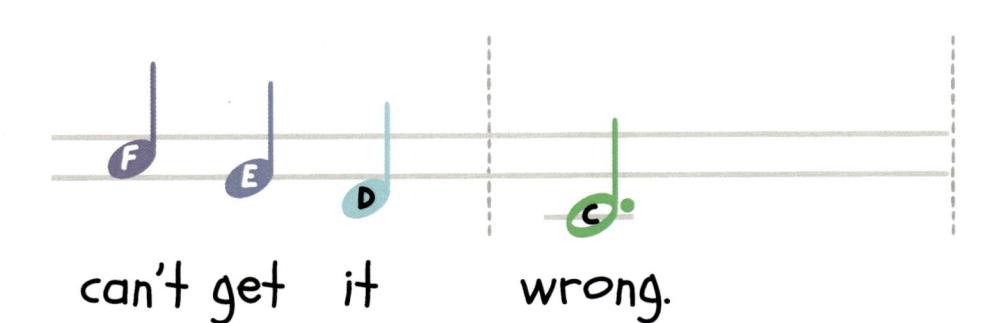

Sing us a song.

We'll sing a - long.

When you're a par-rot you

can't get it wrong.

STEM UP / STEM DOWN MASTERY

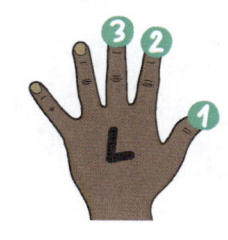

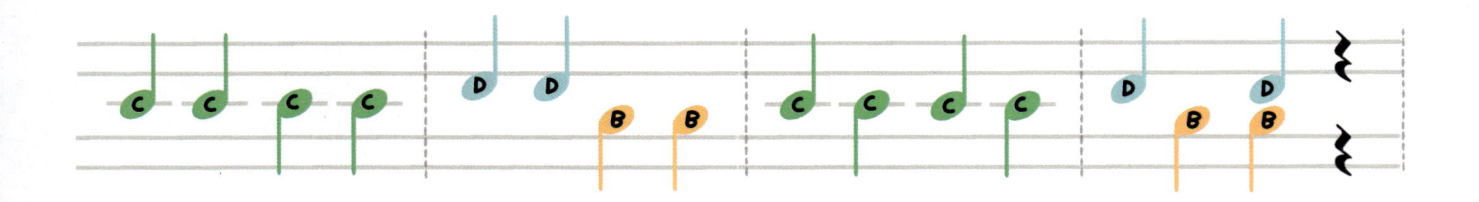

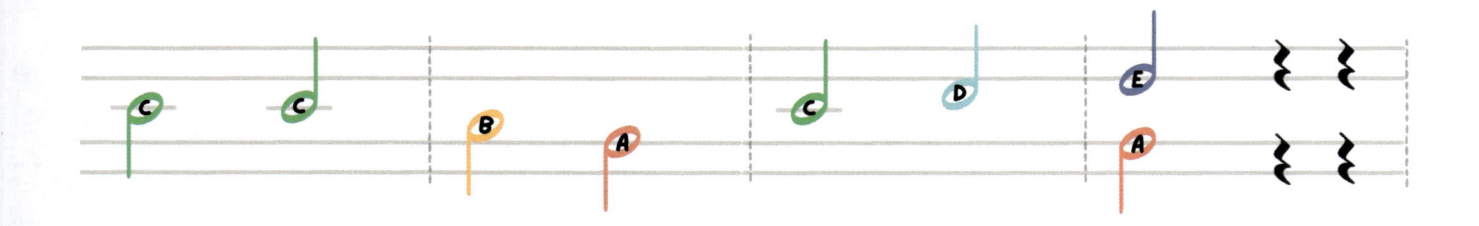

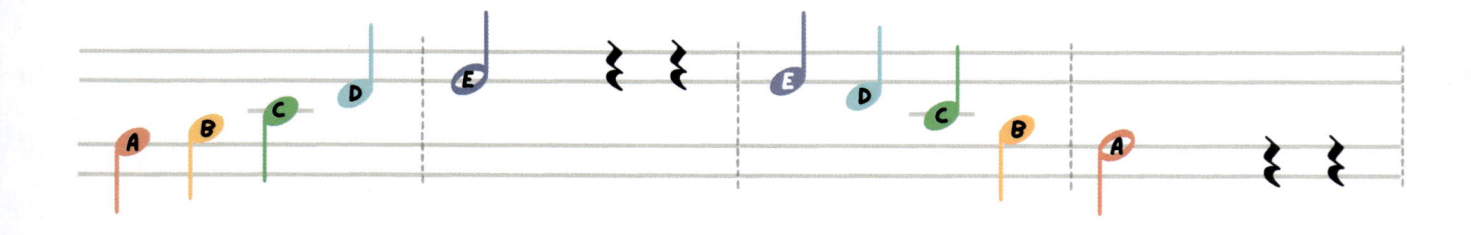

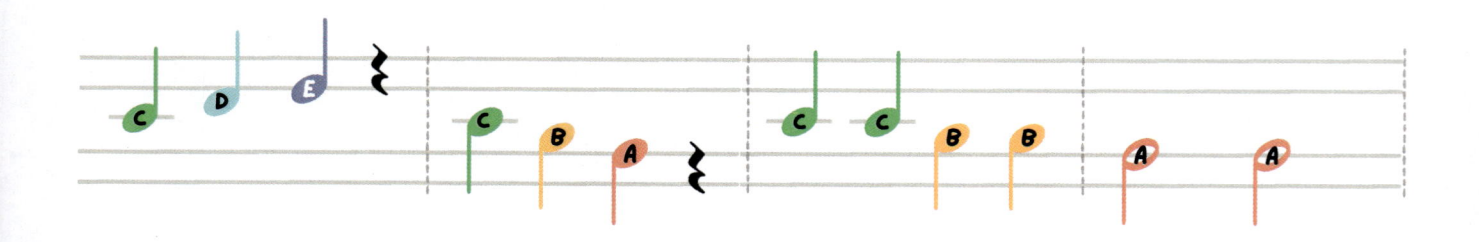

STEPS & SKIPS ON THE KEYS

NEW SKILL 11

STEP
F G
The **NEXT** white key up or down.
(next letter of the alphabet)

SKIP
F A
Skips over **ONE** white key.
(skips one letter of the alphabet)

YOUR TURN:

PLAY EVERY KEY GOING UP BY STEP (START ON THE LEFT).

A B C D E F G A B C D E F G A B C D E F G A B C D E F G A B C D E F G A B C D E F G A B C D E F G A B C

PLAY THE KEYS GOING UP BY SKIP (START ON THE LEFT).

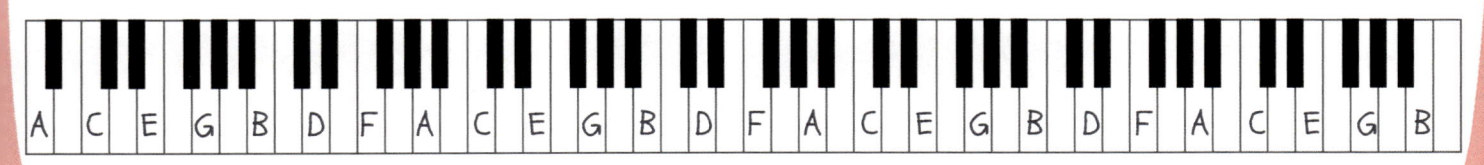

A C E G B D F A C E G B D F A C E G B D F A C E G B

Now repeat these exercises going the other way (start on the right).

LEFT HAND SKIPS

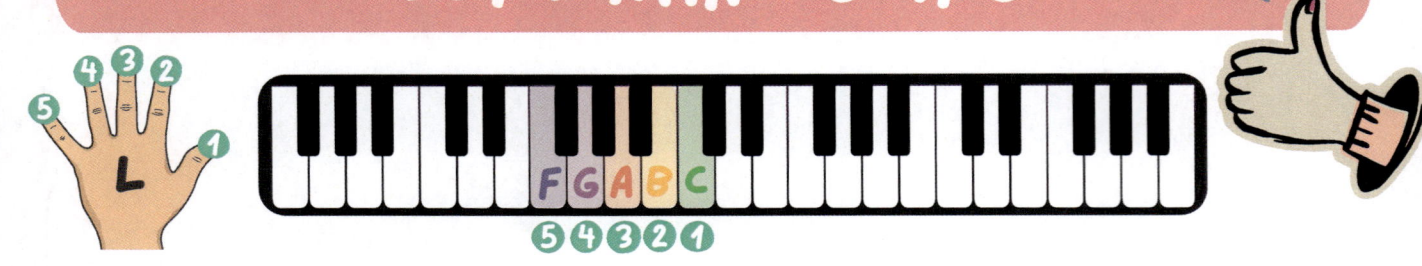

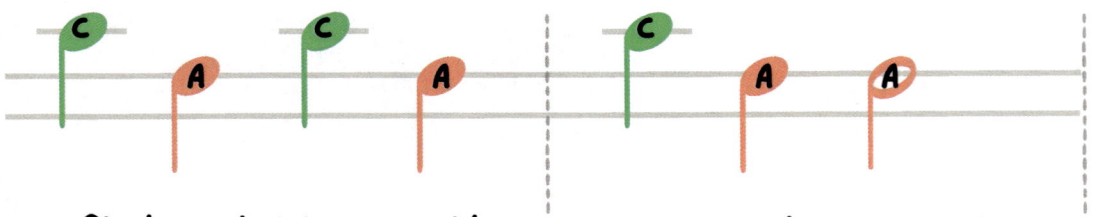

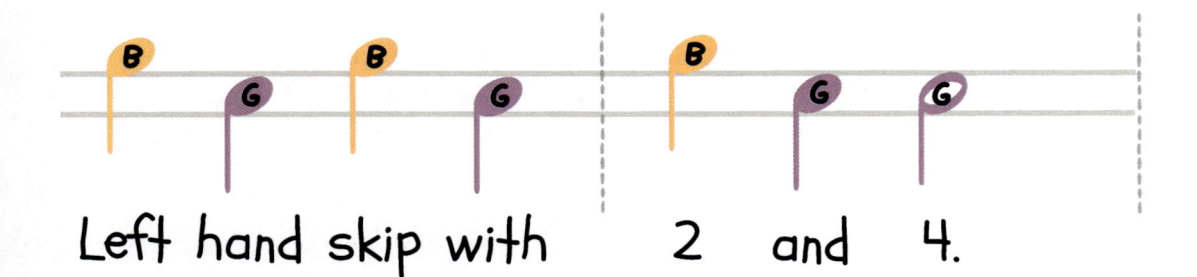

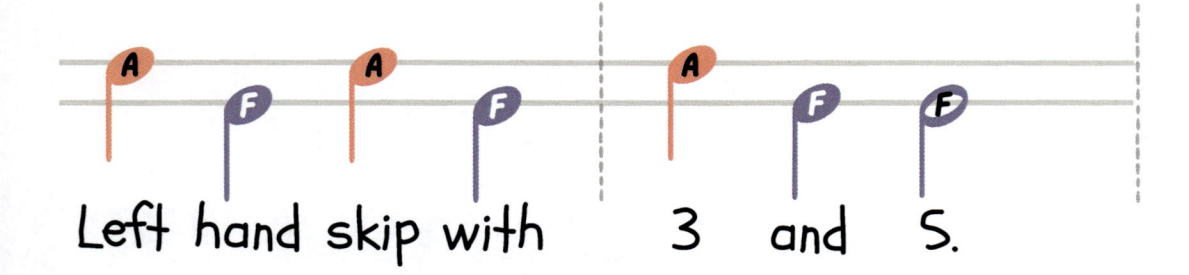

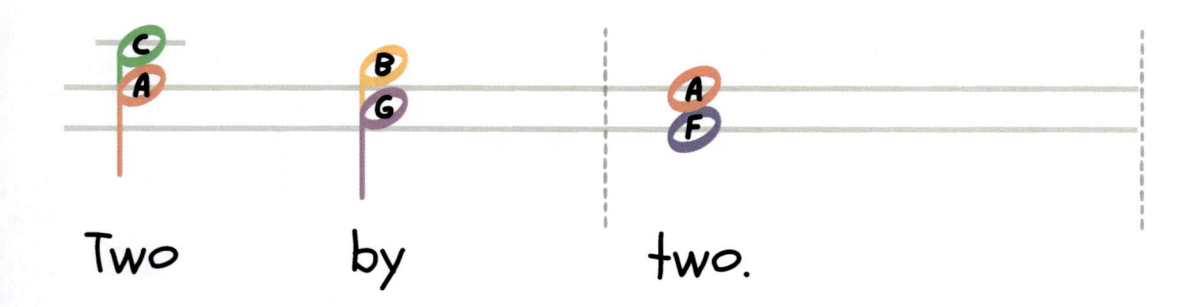

Left hand skip with 1 and 3.

Left hand skip with 2 and 4.

Left hand skip with 3 and 5.

Two by two.

RIGHT HAND SKIPS

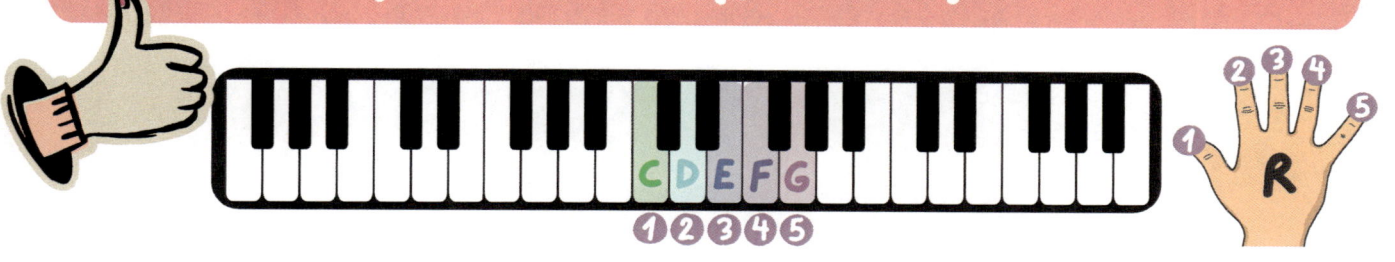

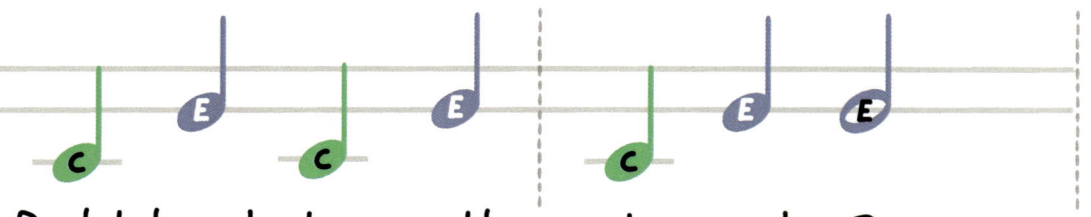

Right hand skip with 1 and 3.

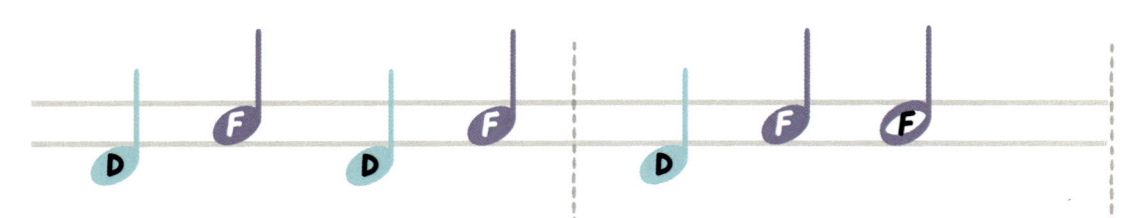

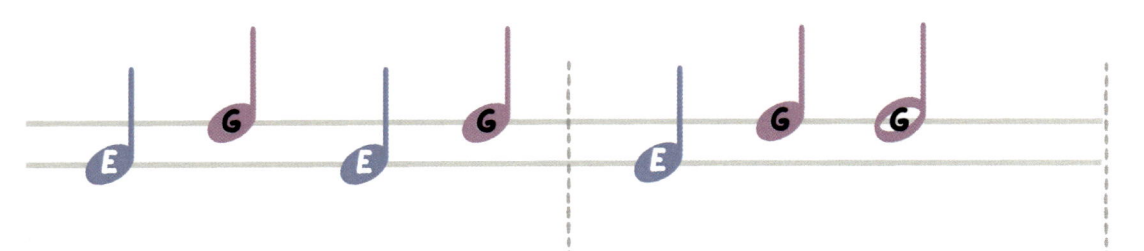

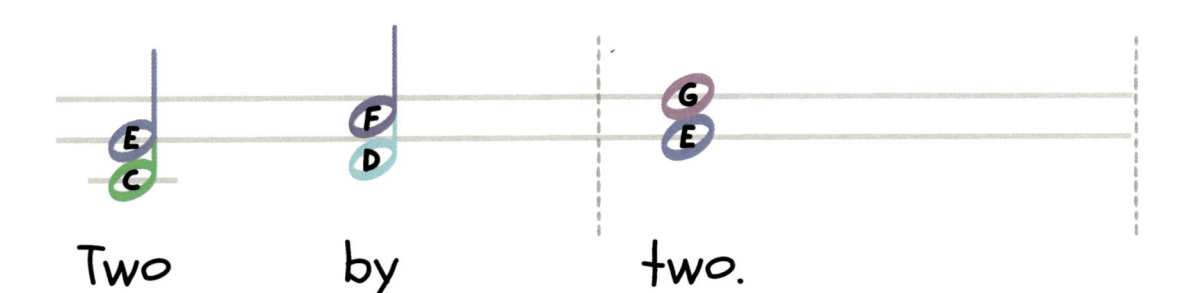

Right hand skip with 2 and 4.

Right hand skip with 3 and 5.

Two by two.

STEPS MASTERY

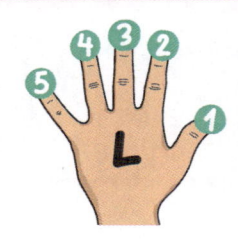

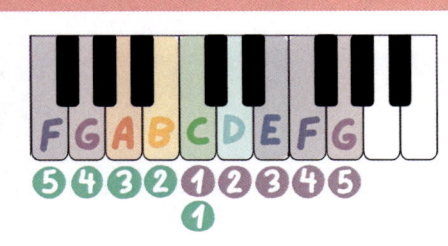

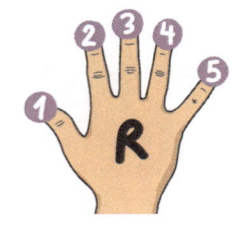

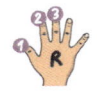

1. MASTER THIS **RIGHT** HAND PATTERN: 3 2 1 2 3

2. MASTER THIS **LEFT** HAND PATTERN: 1 2 3 2 1

3. NOW, MASTER THE PATTERN HANDS TOGETHER.

| E | D | C | D | E |
| C | B | A | B | C |

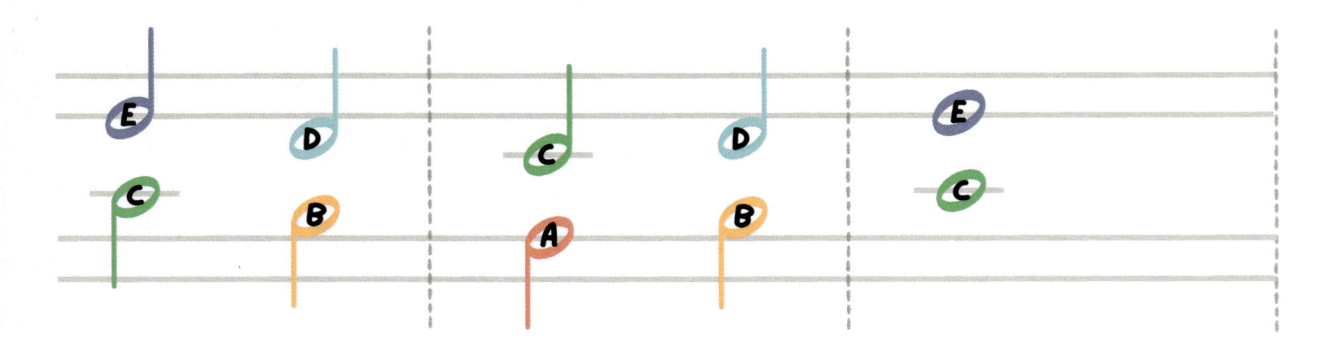

SKIPS MASTERY

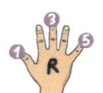

1. MASTER THIS **RIGHT** HAND PATTERN: 5 3 1 3 5

2. MASTER THIS **LEFT** HAND PATTERN: 1 3 5 3 1

3. NOW, MASTER THE PATTERN HANDS TOGETHER.

| G | E | C | E | G |
| C | A | F | A | C |

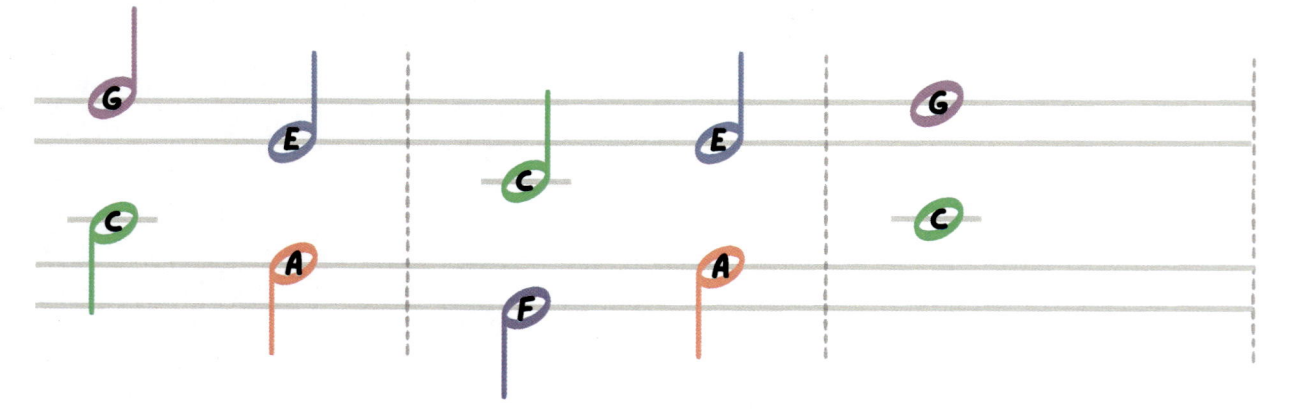

LET'S PLAY: MATCH A SKIP

49

Cut along all dotted lines. Mix up the pieces. Have the student match two notes that are a SKIP apart. Once a match has been found, the student will play the two notes on the piano. (Remember the stem rule.)

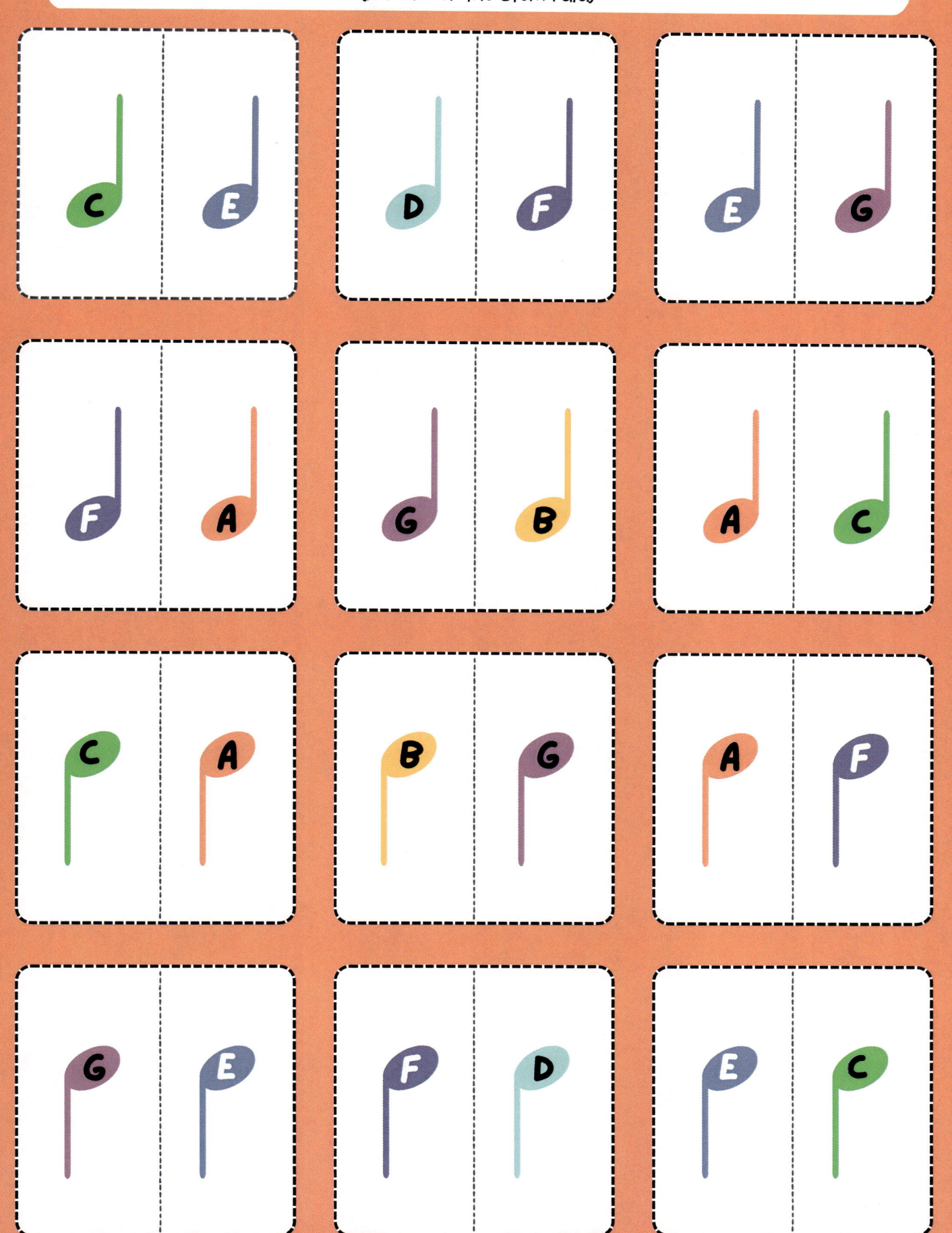

C	E	D	F	E	G
F	A	G	B	A	C
C	A	B	G	A	F
G	E	F	D	E	C

50

UP & DOWN STEPWISE PATTERNS

NEW SKILL 12

MOVING UP
Notes get **HIGHER**.

MOVING DOWN
Notes get **LOWER**.

We read music from LEFT to RIGHT.

YOUR TURN:

PLAY EACH PATTERN. CIRCLE "MOVING UP" OR "MOVING DOWN."

CIRCLE ONE:
- moving up
- moving down

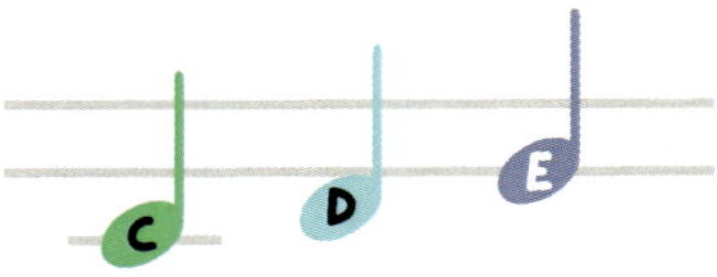

(C, D, E)

CIRCLE ONE:
- moving up
- moving down

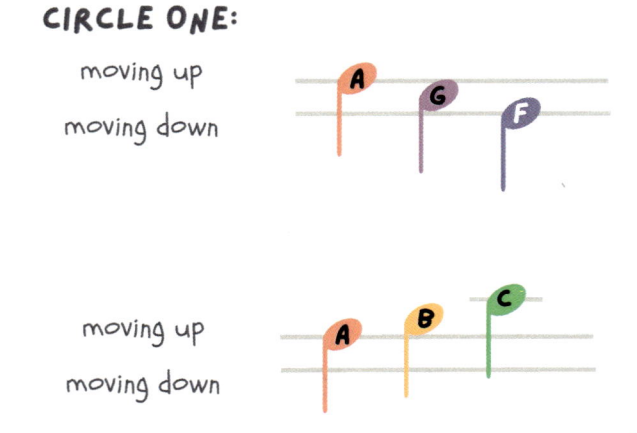

(A, G, F)

- moving up
- moving down

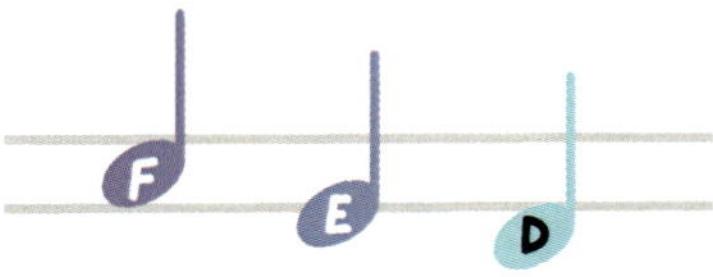

(F, E, D)

- moving up
- moving down

(A, B, C)

52 | RHYTHMIC PATTERNS | NEW SKILL 13

RHYTHM PATTERN

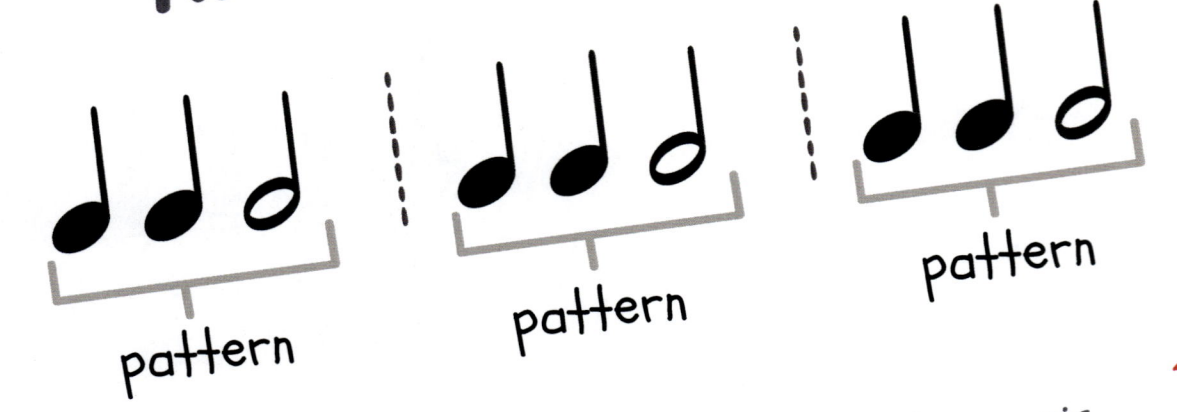

♩ ♩ ♩ | ♩ ♩ ♩ | ♩ ♩ ♩
pattern   pattern   pattern

We can look for repeating PATTERNS in the music.

YOUR TURN:

PLAY THIS PATTERN ON C. NOW ON D. AND NOW ON E.

♩ ♩ ♩ | ♩ ♩ ♩ | ♩ ♩ ♩ | ♩ ♩ ♩

PLAY THIS PATTERN ON B. NOW ON A. AND NOW ON G.

♩ ♩ ♩ 𝄽 | ♩ ♩ ♩ 𝄽 | ♩ ♩ ♩ 𝄽 | ♩ ♩ ♩ 𝄽

PATTERN MASTERY

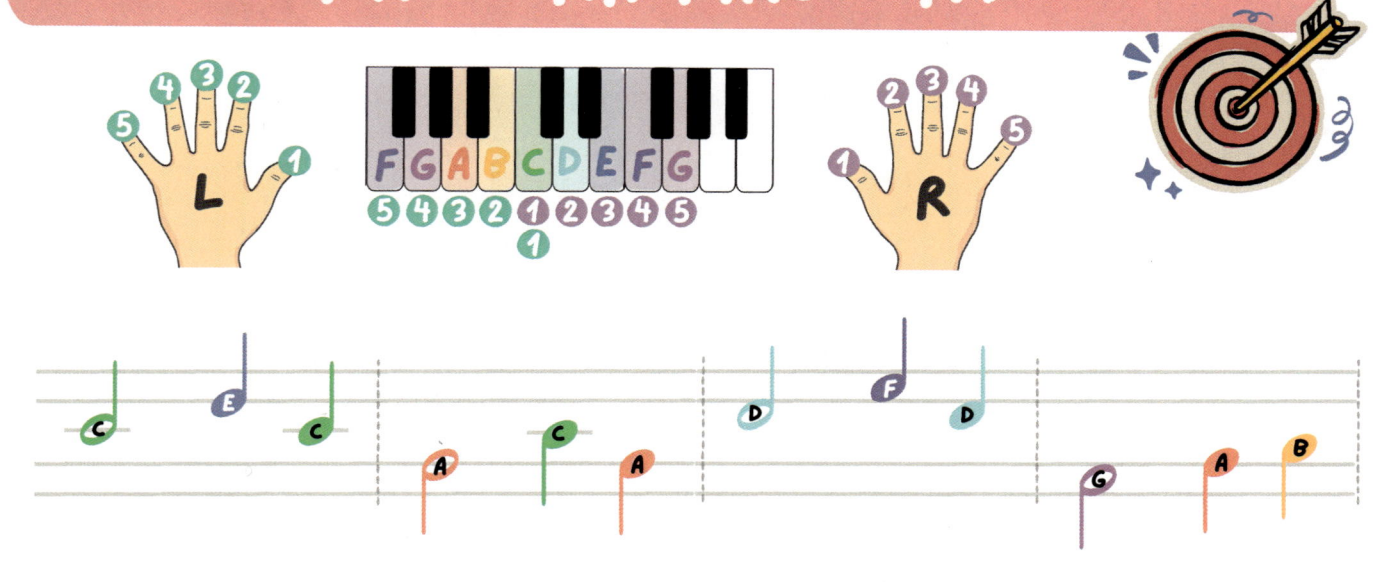

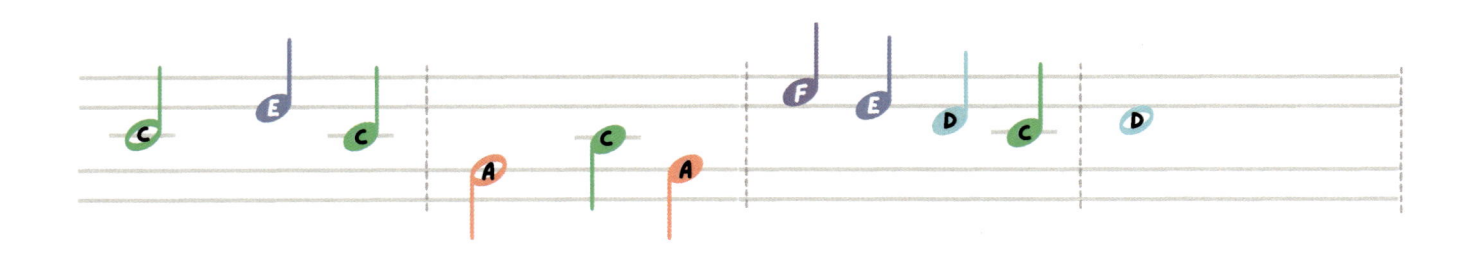

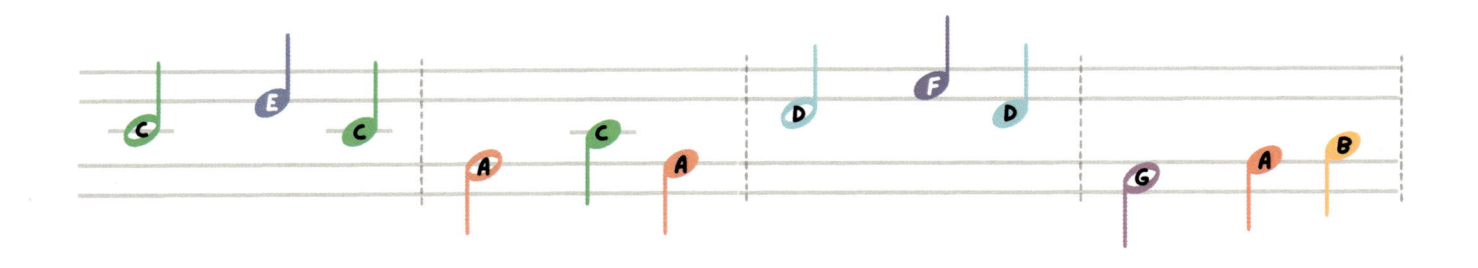

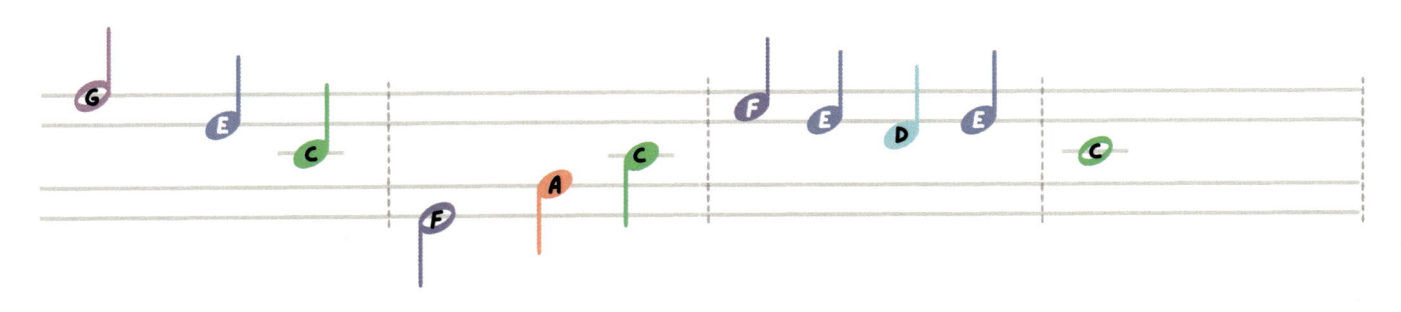

Circle this repeating pattern (there are 12): 𝅗𝅥 ♩ ♩

How many skips can you spot? _____

COMPLETION CERTIFICATE

....
student's name

has successfully completed
Piano Skill Set: Pre-Reading Technique

....
today's date

....
teacher's name

You are now ready for

PIANO SKILL SET PRIMER LEVEL technique

PIANO SKILL SET PRIMER LEVEL writing book

PRIMER LEVEL TECHNIQUE AND WRITING BOOKS